Decisive Parenting

Decisive Parenting

Strategies That WORK with Teenagers

Michael Hammond, PhD

Jason Aronson
Lanham • Boulder • New York • Toronto • Plymouth, UK

This book is intended to present the ideas of the author and others. If the reader requires professional intervention, he or she should consult a competent professional. The author and publisher disclaim liability for any adverse effects resulting directly or indirectly from information contained in this book.

Published by Jason Aronson
An imprint of Rowman & Littlefield Publishers, Inc.
A wholly owned subsidiary of The Rowman & Littlefield Publishing Group, Inc.
4501 Forbes Boulevard, Suite 200, Lanham, Maryland 20706
http://www.rowmanlittlefield.com

Estover Road, Plymouth PL6 7PY, United Kingdom

British Library Cataloguing in Publication Information Available

Library of Congress Cataloging-in-Publication Data

Hammond, Michael.
  Decisive parenting : strategies that work with teenagers / Michael Hammond.
    p. cm.
  Includes bibliographical references and index.
  ISBN 978-0-7657-0763-5 (cloth : alk. paper) — ISBN 978-0-7657-0765-9 (electronic)
  1. Parenting. 2. Parent and teenager—Vocational guidance. I. Title.
HQ755.8.H3335 2010
649'.125—dc22   2009047328

Printed in the United States of America

For Kaitlyn—to the moon and back

CONTENTS

Acknowledgments   ix
How to Use This Book   xi

PART ONE
BUILDING A SECURE FOUNDATION   1

    CHAPTER ONE Rules: Establishing a Firm Foundation   3

    CHAPTER TWO Write the Rules for Your Teenager   9

    CHAPTER THREE Natural and Logical Consequences   21

    CHAPTER FOUR Active Consequences for Challenging
    Situations   28

    CHAPTER FIVE Level Systems, Point Economies, and
    Contracts   50

    CHAPTER SIX Communication That Gets the Results
    You Want   66

    CHAPTER SEVEN Conflict Resolution with Teenagers   87

    CHAPTER EIGHT Reinforcers for Behaviors You Want
    to See Repeated   93

CONTENTS

PART TWO
PROBLEM BEHAVIORS AND WHAT TO DO ABOUT THEM   107

CHAPTER NINE Arguing   109

CHAPTER TEN Chore Completion   115

CHAPTER ELEVEN Driving   121

CHAPTER TWELVE Drug and Alcohol Use   126

CHAPTER THIRTEEN Friends   134

CHAPTER FOURTEEN Information Technology   140

CHAPTER FIFTEEN Lying   144

CHAPTER SIXTEEN Running Away   148

CHAPTER SEVENTEEN School Assignments and
Homework   155

CHAPTER EIGHTEEN Sexual Activity   161

CHAPTER NINETEEN Sibling Fighting   166

CHAPTER TWENTY Stealing   171

CHAPTER TWENTY-ONE Swearing   175

CHAPTER TWENTY-TWO Television   180

CHAPTER TWENTY-THREE Tobacco Use   184

CHAPTER TWENTY-FOUR Truancy   188

CHAPTER TWENTY-FIVE Violence   192

CHAPTER TWENTY-SIX Whereabouts and Curfews   197

Epilogue: Every Good Thing   201
Suggested Reading   203
Index   205
About the Author   209

ACKNOWLEDGMENTS

*D*ecisive Parenting reflects the ideas of a number of people who work as parent training researchers and parent educators and of many parents. All have contributed enormously to this book with their ideas, creativity, dedication, and energy. In particular, I acknowledge the work of Gregory Bodenhamer, George Howard, Dr. J. Douglas Meyer, Dr. Patricia Chamberlain, Dr. David Rimm, Dr. John Masters, Dr. Gerald Patterson, Dr. Alan Kazdin, and Dr. Scott Sells. I would like to thank those who read and commented on earlier drafts of the book, including Dr. Blair Irvine, Dr. Henry Raymond, Dr. Dennis Wong, Dr. Patricia Murphy, Dr. Bill Martin, and Dr. Kevin McMahan. Special thanks are extended to Dr. Lawrence J. Ryan. Any errors that remain are mine.

Lastly, I wish to express my love, appreciation, and thanks to my wife, Trish, and our daughter, Kaitlyn, and to the memory of my parents.

HOW TO USE THIS BOOK

*D*ecisive Parenting is for *any* parent of a teenager, with special reference for parents with kids who are difficult to parent. It is for parents who want specific, concrete skills and answers about how to handle many challenging situations and circumstances with teenagers.

The book is written with a four-fold purpose:

- to help you improve your relationship with your teenager

- to give you the tools to *stop* misbehavior

- to show you how to encourage positive behavior

- to help you guide teenagers to become responsible and trustworthy adults

In my parenting classes, there are parents who say, "I don't have any major behavior problems, which you say you'll cover, but I do have some minor things, like having my kids do chores and homework. I'd really like some help with that." Other parents say, "Dr. Hammond, I have all the big problems—arguing, running away from home, drugs—all of it. I desperately need help because I can't find any parenting classes or books that help with all the stuff she's into!" And then there are the parents who tell me, "I came to your workshop because I want to know how to prevent problems later on, *before* they start. We're doing okay right now. What can I do to keep it that way?"

Decisive Parenting is full of tools and skills for every level of difficulty with teenagers, from minor irritations to major disconnection between child and parent. Regardless if your teenager is heaven sent or hell bent, this book can help you. Keep in mind, however, that not *every* skill is for *every* parent. You'll need to choose according to your situation. You can do this several ways:

- Read the book cover to cover, using all of the skills that apply to your situation.

- Read the part you like and apply those skills; disregard what you do not like.

- Use the book like a toolbox; take it out when you need an answer to a problem.

Part I covers behavioral tools that help families function well. You will learn how to construct rules and consequences that are consistently effective. Part I also covers communication, encouragement, and active problem solving. By using these skills collectively, you will be able to guide and direct your teenager through the adolescent years with great success.

Part II presents time-tested solutions to a variety of problems, some simple and minor (but no less irritating and disruptive to family functioning) and some serious enough to threaten your teenager's safety and the parent-child relationship. Choose what you think is relevant to you and what you find useful.

The most important thing is to know that you *can* change how things are going in your home and with your teenager. *Believe* that you can, put your trust in the skills you are about to learn, and apply them with ever-increasing confidence. Do this and you will see the results you want. I have taught thousands of parents to use these skills and tools effectively. They can be just as successful for you.

**Please note that there are several worksheets referred to within the text that can be downloaded from the companion website for this book, decisiveparenting.com. These items are as follows:

Discipline Plan Worksheet
Rules Tracking Guide
Problem Behavior Checklist
Problem-Solving Worksheet
Daily Class Assignment Report
School Behavior Checklist
Community Behavior Checklist

Part One
BUILDING A SECURE FOUNDATION

RULES: ESTABLISHING A FIRM FOUNDATION

Rules are basic to family life. Rules establish the firm foundation for a discipline plan. Establish firm and fair rules, and discipline will follow naturally from them.

Rules are best when they are based on your family's values—the standards you believe are important to follow. Such rules provide a moral compass that helps your teenager find his way.

When rules for teenagers are unclear, unnecessary, unfair, or unenforceable, anger and chaos quickly develop. The *absence of clear expectations* causes friction between you because your teenager doesn't know what you expect of him. So rules need to be constructed deliberately and carefully. Before we begin to construct rules, let's see what a rule is or is not.

Definition of a Rule

A rule is different from a *hope*. "I wish that you would do all of your homework before going out" says you would *prefer* that he do the homework.

A *demand* is more like a rule: "You will do all of your homework before going out." However, a demand, such as this, is personal and sets up a power struggle with your teenager.

An *expectation* is not demanding enough. "I expect that you'll do all of your homework before going out" provides no consequences other than failure to meet the expectation.

"Before you go out, complete all of your homework every night that it's assigned" is a *rule*. It tells the teenager what to do and when to do it.

So the first thing to know about establishing rules is that you want to avoid stating a hope, a desire, a personal demand, or an expectation. A rule tells exactly what and when you expect your adolescent to do something. Rules are the home's version of society's laws that regulate public behavior. None of us can do as we please whenever we like—good rules, like good laws, prevent chaos.

"Rules" for Developing Rules

There are five rules, or principles, for the *development* of a rule.

1. Focus on behavior, not attitudes.

2. Write down the rule; say it aloud often.

3. Tie the rule to a set consequence.

4. Involve your kids in devising rules.

5. Monitor compliance with the rule consistently.

Rule 1: Focus on Behavior, Not Attitudes

Behavior can be seen or detected. You can see that your teenager cleaned her room, fed the dog, or did not come home intoxicated. You can see by the evidence of her *behavior* if she has complied with a rule about cleaning her bedroom, feeding the dog, or drinking alcohol.

You cannot see or have a clear understanding of her *attitude* about complying with the rule. She may not *like* the necessary behavior or your demand to stop the prohibited behavior, but that is not the issue. The issue is whether or not she is in compliance with the rule—regardless of how she feels about it. When she is in compliance, be sure to praise her and encourage her—which goes a long way toward helping most people change their attitudes.

Having a rule such as "improve your attitude toward your sister" is pointless. What is it that you want your teenager to do or not do? How will he or you know that he has done it? If you want him to stop hitting his sister, you need to say that. A rule such as "never hit your sister" focuses on the behavior that you can see or detect and not on an attitude that you cannot see.

Rule 2: Write Down the Rule

Rules are much more likely to be observed when we write them down. You can post them in final form in a prominent place, such as on the refrigerator or the bathroom door. Give your teenager a copy of the rules, retaining your own copy. This procedure prevents arguments later over exactly what the rules state. If there is a dispute about who does dishes on Mondays and Wednesdays—or is it Mondays and Thursdays?—you have the written form to refresh everyone's memory.

It's a good idea to repeat the rule as necessary. You can say, "The rule is: 'Wash all the dinner dishes every night that you're assigned.'" Your kids will likely pick up on this quickly and say, "Yeah, I know, the rule is: 'Wash all the dinner @#$%^ dishes every night that you're assigned.' You don't have to tell me." That's just fine because your teenager has internalized the rule—even if he or she doesn't like it.

You can write the rules down and repeat them to your teenager until you're blue in the face, but if there is no follow-up on the rule, it is a colossal waste of time and energy. To help you follow up, you'll need to tie the rule to a set consequence.

Rule 3: Tie the Rule to a Set Consequence

When teenagers know beforehand that if they choose to break or disregard a rule an unpleasant consequence will follow, they are much more likely to follow the rule. But too often kids choose to gamble. They gamble that they can get by with breaking the rule, or that you will likely not enforce it. Sometimes they gamble and lose. That is when you find out about the wrongdoing and decide to discipline your teenager. But often your teenager can get by with a warning, or get through the confrontation with pleas, yelling, threats, and promises. This brand of inconsistency breeds contempt for rules and for discipline when it does come.

A more effective alternative is to clearly identify what your teenager will lose if she chooses to gamble on rule enforcement in the first place. Don't let her guess. Don't hope that you can think of some really good consequence after the fact. Instead, clearly identify the consequence that is built into the rule.

With this method, your teenager has certain knowledge that if she chooses to break the rule, she is choosing the consequence that is part and parcel of the rule. This helps her develop consequential thinking, a critical skill, for now she knows if she chooses to do A, B will follow as surely as night follows day. I call these rules "consequence rules," and they are the only type of rule you'll need. Here are two examples:

Rule: Put all dirty clothes into the hamper.

Consequence: Clothes that are not in the hamper will not be washed.

Rule: Finish your homework every night that it is assigned.

Consequence: Stay home that evening to finish uncompleted homework.

We will explore in depth what kind of consequences to use and how to enforce them in later chapters.

Rule 4: Involve Your Teenager in Devising Rules

It is a good idea to involve your teenager in devising new rules and changing old ones as necessary. People take much better care of things they have a hand in constructing than things they haven't.

Sit down with your adolescent and explain your concerns about a particular behavior and the need for a rule to change the behavior. Ask for her input and opinion. Some kids cannot or will not participate in this process. If your teenager refuses to have input, tell her that's fine; you'll go ahead without her. Then go ahead. Most kids will quickly realize it is to their advantage to be involved, because they are more likely to have the rule turn out to their liking. The advantage to you as the parent is that you'll likely get considerably less resistance to the rule when your teenager is directly involved in its construction.

Rule 5: Monitor Compliance with the Rule Consistently

Consistency is the key to success in establishing and gaining compliance with rules. A rule will quickly float away like a breeze on a hot night if the parent enforces the rule one day and disregards it the next.

Teenagers learn very quickly from experience that the rule is of little value and can be safely ignored. They will think, "Mom and Dad don't really care about enforcing the rule, so why should I be concerned about following it?"

Consider the family where the teenager is told to be home by a set curfew. She is compliant for a day or two. On the third day she decides to test the rule and comes home half an hour late. Her parent gives her a dirty look and tells her always to be home by curfew. The teenager is home by curfew the next three nights, and then she stays out two hours late on the fourth night. Her parent yells and threatens. She stays out two hours late the next night. This time her parent looks at her in disgust and doesn't say anything about the curfew rule. Thereafter, the teenager stays out as late as she likes. And the rule? With no consequence or enforcement, the rule has drifted away on the night air.

How Many Rules Do You Need?

Some families have a difficult time because they have too many rules. When there are too many, the importance and need for any one rule is lost in a sea of regulation. Kids don't need a rule for every behavior under the sun. Parents who try to micromanage every aspect of their kids' behavior day and night invite rebellion.

It is very hard for both parents and teenagers to keep track of multiple rules. However, it can be disastrous to have too few rules, or worse yet, no rules. The solution is to have a few rules, ones that are necessary, fair, clear, enforceable, and consistently applied.

Sunset Rules

Rules should have a beginning and an end. You wouldn't think of having the same rules for crossing the street for your fifteen-year-old as you would for your five-year-old. When a rule is no longer needed, it should die a natural death. Either circumstances or your experience with the teenager make the rule unnecessary. I call these rules "sunset rules" in that they have a "sunset clause" when the need for the rule has passed. However, some rules will be in effect in one form or another for years—rules about attending school or completing chores, for example. When do these rules formally sunset? When your son or daughter is no longer living at home or is no longer dependent on you, the rule sunsets.

Now we are ready for the task of deciding what rules your family needs and learning how to construct them so that they will provide a secure foundation for the parent-child relationship. If your rules are weak or nonexistent, hang on. Help is here!

CHAPTER TWO
WRITE THE RULES FOR YOUR TEENAGER

There are four essential *characteristics* of a rule. A rule needs to be necessary, fair, clear, and enforceable. To make it enforceable, we combine it with a known consequence. First, however, let's talk about how to make sure the rule is necessary, fair, and clear.

Necessary Rules

A rule is necessary when there is a difficult or problematic or unacceptable behavior that needs to change. A teenager who skips school twice in the course of the school year does not have the same level of problem behavior as one who skips every week. If a teenager fails a test once in a blue moon, that is one thing; if she habitually chooses to fail all of her tests, that is something else entirely. In the first instance, you can handle the problem without a rule. In the second instance, you certainly do need a rule about schoolwork and preparing for tests.

The yardstick to measure the need is the *frequency and intensity* of the problem behavior. How often does the behavior occur? How big a problem is the behavior when it does occur? Behaviors that occur frequently and are intense are good candidates for modification through rules.

Fair Rules

A rule needs to be fair to be effective. When it comes to rules they don't like, kids frequently say, "That's not fair!" which can be translated, "That's not the way I want it to be." By fairness I mean it is something that the teenager is capable of doing. A four-year-old cannot be expected to clean her room to a high standard; a fourteen-year-old certainly can. A fair rule is also with the bounds of common sense. It is neither fair nor reasonable nor likely to happen when we have a rule that a teenager will do four hours of homework every night, especially when she has never done a minute of homework a day in her life.

A rule is especially fair when one person's behavior directly affects the rights of others and is for the common good. Fairness often depends upon your perspective. A teenager may say, "I should be able to keep my room any way I want—it's my room." However, a rule about keeping a clean room is fair because the bedroom is connected to the rest of the house that everyone shares. An unkempt bedroom may be an eyesore, as well as a health and safety concern. (If it's not, or you really don't care how the kids keep their rooms, don't make such a rule.)

There are different rules and expectations for different people at different ages and under different circumstances. Your five-year-old will not get to do or have certain things that a ten-year-old will; likewise the sixteen-year-old. With more freedom come more choices, and also more responsibility to make appropriate choices. Your thirteen-year-old doesn't get to have sex, drink alcohol, or drive a car. But you do if you choose. The rules for you are different. While this may not seem fair to teenagers, they learn to put up with these differences.

Clear Rules

A rule must be clear to be effective. The best way to be clear is to use words that describe behavior. The rule "never get drunk at parties" seems clear until you think about it carefully. You may have a clear idea of what you mean, but your teenager may or may not. The rule is subject to interpretation as follows:

> *Never*—Never is fine. Never means never.
> *Get drunk*—Do you want your teenager not to drink alcohol, or just not to get drunk when he does?
> *At parties*—Can he drink in the car with his friends? In his room? At school?

With this unclear rule, your teenager can drink alcohol to the point of intoxication anywhere at any time with anyone and still comply perfectly with the rule, provided he does not get drunk at parties. "Never drink alcohol until you are of legal age" is a much clearer rule.

Teenagers are frequently Philadelphia lawyers and are looking for loopholes that allow them to interpret a rule to their advantage. The easiest way to avoid misinterpretation is to write the rule simply and clearly.

Enforceable Rules

A rule on drinking alcohol is fine, but is pointless if it is not enforced or is unenforceable. Devising a rule will not necessarily alter your teenager's behavior any more than a posted speed limit will deter speeders. After one or two speeding tickets, however, most of us will hold the speed down, at least on the section of road where we got the ticket. So it is with kids. Teenagers need consistent sanctions for breaking the rule. But when sanctions are given sporadically, or not at all, the teenager learns that he can get by with breaking the rule. He then strives to find out each time if this is a time he can get by with breaking the rule. A rule based on behavior you can see can be enforced with consequences. A consequence is the thing that happens next after you choose a behavior, and all behavior has consequences.

Watch Your Language When Writing Rules

A rule can be necessary, fair, clear, and enforceable and still crack and creak like a foundation infested with termites. There are some important guidelines to follow when writing rules that will help prevent failure before you even begin.

One of the greatest weaknesses in the rule occurs when it is constructed using accusatory or demeaning language. Directives like "Because you're such a pig, always clean up your room" and "Since we can't trust you, come home from school immediately" are disrespectful and do nothing to build a positive relationship between you and your teenager.

Using authoritarian language in the rule will likely invite a power struggle. Rules that begin with the word *you* are authoritarian: "You will," "You shall," and "You must." Listen: "You shall be home by 9 o'clock every night"; "You will do all of your homework every night it's assigned"; "You must take out the trash can to the curb every Monday night." Teenagers, like everyone else, are usually more cooperative when they believe they are being treated with respect, instead of being ordered around like drones.

Now listen to the revised rules: "Be home by 9 o'clock every night"; "Do all of your homework every night that it's assigned"; "Take out the trash can to the curb every Monday night." The rules have lost none of their clarity or authority. Your teenager still may not want to do the task, but she is less likely to feel personally offended by the rule. The word "you" makes the rule personal. Depending on how I feel about you and you about me, I am likely to take that into consideration when I hear "you" in the rule: "Oh yeah? We'll just see if I do it or not. They can't tell me what to do!"

Notice that none of these rules is a request or a desire. They are requirements. Requirements are not offensive in and of themselves. If we want something to happen, we must meet the requirements. A teenager will not graduate unless she meets the requirements of the school. He must meet the requirements to obtain a driver's license. If she wants to play sports, she must follow the requirements to participate. If he wants a job, he must meet the employer's requirements. We all must meet the requirements to do or have certain things throughout our lives. And there is nothing wrong with parents requiring certain behaviors from their teenagers.

There is also nothing wrong with stating requests or desires to your teenager. A request or desire gives your teenager the option of doing something or not doing it; there is a choice. For example, "Would you fix dinner for the family tonight?" is a request; your teenager may answer, "No, I'm too tired from play practices all week." A rule, in contrast, offers no choice.

Notice that in the examples above, each rule has one behavior. A rule such as "Take out the trash can to the curb every Monday night, and then come back in and sweep out the garage, and then empty the cat box, and then go back into the house and do all of your homework before watching TV" is confusing and burdensome. If you want the behaviors behind each of these rules altered because they are a consistent problem, you'll need a separate rule for each behavior.

To summarize, there are four guidelines for the language you should use when writing a rule:

- Leave out accusatory or demeaning language.
- Do not begin a rule with *you* as that invites a power struggle.
- Do not write a request or a desire.
- Focus on one behavior per rule.

Writing Rules

A good way to start a rule is to use either an action word, such as "go," "clean," "begin," or a time element, such as "When you come home from school . . ." or "As soon as you are out of bed in the morning . . ." or "By 6:30 each evening . . ." Another good way is to use the words "always" and "never," as in "always do . . ." or "never do . . ."

Use plain, simple language that anyone can understand. Be short and to the point. Focus on the one behavior that you want to see and nothing else. Finally, only use the words *always* and *never* when you mean exactly that. Otherwise these words will quickly lose their effectiveness.

Practice writing out the rules you want and saying them out loud. Ask others if they think the rules sounds right, and if they think the proposed rule will do what you want it to do. Watch for loopholes or how the rule can be misinterpreted.

Here are a few representative rules that parents have constructed in my parenting classes. See if you can pick out the ones that meet all of the rule criteria (especially the ones that are necessary, fair, clear, and enforceable) and which ones need an overhaul.

Act your age.
Go to school.
Do what you're told.
Attend every class every day school is in session.
Don't talk so long on the phone.
Stop arguing.
Always ask permission before using my tools.
Do four hours of homework every night.

Limit your calls to ten minutes and three calls an evening.
Never argue, discuss.
Stop hanging around those people.
Spend money wisely.
Stop hitting your brother.
Do your chores.

These are the "good" rules from the list that meet all of the criteria:

Attend every class every day school is in session.
Always ask permission before using my tools.
Limit your calls to ten minutes and three calls an evening.
Never argue, discuss.

Because of the way they are constructed, the others are unclear ("Act your age"), unnecessary ("Spend money wisely"), unfair ("Do what you're told"), or unreasonable ("Do four hours of homework every night"). Some of the rules have all four problems.

Write Your Own Rules for Your Teenager

1. Make a list of the problems you're having with your teenager. (For help, refer to the "Problem Behavior Checklist" on page 16; this checklist is also provided on the website.) Use action words (behavior you can see). Write down as many problems as occur to you. Do not try to analyze or come to a conclusion about *why* your teenager acts that way, just write down the problem.
2. Review your whole list, considering the *frequency and intensity* of each problem behavior. How often does the problem behavior occur (frequency), and how big a problem is it when the behavior occurs (intensity)?
3. Draw a line through those behaviors that have occurred infrequently or are not so important at this time. Now look at your list. You should have two or three problem behaviors you especially want to work on. If you have four, five, or more, go over the list again and prioritize the top three. These are the ones you want or need to see behavior change on right now.

If you are parenting with someone else, compare your lists. Choose the top three problem behaviors the two of you can agree to work on together with your teenager. If you cannot agree on an item, ask a third party whose opinion you both respect to help you decide. If you still cannot agree about one or more items, ask the other parent to back you up as you work with your teenager on changing that problem behavior. If your partner refuses to help you in any way, you can go it alone, or you can consider eliminating the behavior from your list.

4. Now consider, if you were to construct a rule with a set consequence for noncompliance (the "consequence rule") for each behavior problem you identified, could you make the rule meet these criteria: is it necessary, fair, clear, and enforceable? If not, you may need to rethink the rule in behavioral terms.

5. Sit down with your teenager (if you can) and explain your concerns about his or her behavior using your list of two or three areas. Ask for your teenager's input and opinion.

6. Write a consequence rule using the "Discipline Plan Worksheet" provided on the website. Look the rule over to make sure it deals with one behavior and is clear, fair, reasonable, and enforceable.

7. Tie the rule to a specific consequence or a series of consequences. Accomplish this step collaboratively with your teenager, if possible. (See page 41.)

8. Put the rule into effect; let your teenager know that from now on there is a rule and consequence for not following it. Write down the consequence rule and post it where your teenager will see it regularly.

9. Track compliance with the consequence rule using the "Rules Tracking Guide" provided on the website.

10. Revise or add new consequence rules as you need them, always remembering to have only a few rules at any one time.

Partnership between Parents

Even though your teenager may be cooperative about following rules you construct, what should you do if one parent favors a rule but the other does not?

Problem Behavior Checklist

Make a list of all of the behaviors that your adolescent is currently doing that are a significant problem. Consider the *frequency and intensity* of the problem before you add it to your list. Does the problem behavior occur with increasing frequency, and is the problem intense when it does occur? Add any problem behaviors that are not on the list, but relevant to your situation. Complete a separate list for each teenager whose behavior concerns you.

Around the House:

- leaving dirty clothes/dishes lying around
- getting up too late/staying up too late
- arguing with parents
- arguing or fighting with siblings
- "borrowing" family members' belongings
- misuse of the phone
- not completing chores
- misuse of television, stereo, computer, or electronic games
- unacceptable level of hygiene

School-Related:

- not completing homework
- playing video games instead of doing homework
- failing grades
- skipping school
- wearing gang clothes and insignia

Out and About:

- notification of whereabouts
- coming home after curfew
- staying out overnight without permission
- involvement with a boyfriend or girlfriend
- being sexually active

- misuse of the car
- lying
- running away
- choice of friends/associates
- drug and/or alcohol use
- use of tobacco
- violent behavior
- shoplifting, stealing
- vandalizing property
- other: _____

What should happen if Dad wants a consequence rule for washing dishes after snacks, but Mom doesn't really care? What if Mom wants a consequence rule for drinking alcohol, but Dad doesn't care if the kid has a beer once in a while? Here are some guidelines for you to follow.

- Be sure the rule is not only wanted, but also necessary.

- If it is necessary, is it also clear, fair, reasonable, and written in behavioral terms that everyone can understand?

- Are you willing to take a stand for the rule, and to follow through consistently in enforcing the rule?

If you can arrive at a "yes" for all three of these questions, go forward. Here is what you can do.

The best way for families to work together on establishing rules is to come to *agreement*. You talk and listen to one another with caring concern and agree to take a united stand on the rule. You then seek the input, cooperation, and agreement of your teenager. Most kids will want to have input on the rule. Welcome their input because they are more likely to cooperate if they have a hand in constructing it. When a teenager refuses to have anything to do with rule construction, you say, "Fine, we'll go ahead without you. And the rules still stand." Then go ahead.

If both parents cannot agree on the rule, then the parent who wants the rule must agree to be the primary agent for enforcing the rule. The other parent who doesn't care that strongly about the rule must agree to back up the parent who does feel strongly. The rule may not be what one of you would like, but you're willing to concede to your partner's wishes and support the rule.

Both parents and the teenager may talk over the rule and find areas that can be negotiated and compromised on, while still retaining the essence of the rule. This is coming to an *accommodation* about the rule. A useful alternative is for the parents to contact a third party whose opinion is respected by *both parents* and ask for his or her suggestions. This could be a friend, relative, clergy, a therapist, or Dear Abby. The rule may need to be rewritten at this point. This means coming to a *consensus* about the rule.

Finally, you can *ditch* the rule; do away with it. If both parents cannot work together in any of the ways listed, it is better to give up on the rule and permit your teenager to do as he or she sees fit in this or that behavioral area. This is usually bad policy for your teenager, and it teaches nothing about compliance, discipline, cooperation, and respect. However, it is better than continual family feuding and conflict. Having no rule is also preferable to having a rule that one parent may undermine because he or she doesn't really believe in it. If Mom wants a no-use alcohol rule, and Dad says, "Geez Louise, let the kid have a beer while he is watching the football game," will there likely even be a rule to enforce? If parents regularly disagree on what rules to have, it may mean the family has serious problems. At this point, seek out a family therapist to help sort out the situation.

The best way for families to work together on establishing consequence rules is to come to an agreement. The next best way is to come to an accommodation about the rule. The third way is to come to a consensus. Finally, ditch the rule if there is no other way. In most families where love and caring exist, there is a way. The reason for family rules is because we love our children. Love makes the way.

Reasonable Guidelines as Alternatives to Rules

One last important point about rules. There are a few behaviors where the perspective rule would meet all of the criteria for a consequence rule, but the enforcement of it would be pointless. These are matters of the heart: rules about attending religious services, engaging in charitable work, or the teenager having contact with an absent parent with whom he or she has emotional issues. You will not win your teenager's allegiance by having a rule for these behaviors. You can say what you would *like* to have happen, based upon your values, but this is fundamentally different from the demand through a rule.

Does that mean you should never require your kid to do something he or she might find unpleasant? Of course not. It depends upon the circumstances. You should exercise discretion at times. Likewise, in some cases you can encourage and support your teenager to make the decisions that you would prefer, but will respect her choices, as difficult as that may be for you.

It is also a waste of time to set rules for things that will likely be thrown over for something new. Hairstyles, clothing, music, and other will change as your , clothes, and music, *asonable guidelines* for in those parameters. ored hair. Some kids costume jewelry, and music that will drive hey are back to their tening to 1950s rock. over. Choosing your elines help you avoid For example:

649,125

's as long as it is

here are no refer-
iatan.

to gangsta rap.

like, what you would prefer, but as long as they do no harm, they are harmless. Even if the teenager dresses like a rodeo clown after a rainstorm and listens to music with blasting guitar riffs, screaming incomprehensible lyrics, it is better to let go on these issues than to give on critical issues that do involve your teenager's welfare, safety, or well-being.

Well, what if your teenager's choice does involve his or her welfare, safety, or well-being? For example, should you let your teenager dress like a gangster? Or have contact with adult strangers over the Internet? Or listen to profanity-laced, sexist, and/or racist music? Your teenager could get shot, or sexually assaulted, or have his or her mind polluted. For most parents, this kind of restriction on their teenager's choice comes under the heading of reasonable guidelines. You may need to set limits and veto choices over the limits, but if you do, be prepared to monitor and supervise compliance. It may not be easy. Saying no and meaning it rarely is.

In chapters 3 and 4, I show you how to choose an effective consequence, tie it to the rule, and to enforce it. Rules rule!

the teenager having contact with an absent parent with whom he or she has emotional issues. You will not win your teenager's allegiance by having a rule for these behaviors. You can say what you would *like* to have happen, based upon your values, but this is fundamentally different from the demand through a rule.

Does that mean you should never require your kid to do something he or she might find unpleasant? Of course not. It depends upon the circumstances. You should exercise discretion at times. Likewise, in some cases you can encourage and support your teenager to make the decisions that you would prefer, but will respect her choices, as difficult as that may be for you.

It is also a waste of time to set rules for things that will likely be thrown over for something new. Hairstyles, clothing, music, and other things that involve personal taste and preference will change as your teenager gets older. You could set rules for hairstyle, clothes, and music, but what would be the point? Instead, you can set *reasonable guidelines* for your teenager to follow. He or she may choose within those parameters. Yes, some kids will choose spiked, kaleidoscope-colored hair. Some kids will want to combine gaudy makeup, ragged clothes, costume jewelry, and combat boots. And some kids will want to listen to music that will drive their parents up the wall—and then the next week they are back to their own hair color, wearing conventional clothes, and listening to 1950s rock. By the time you are ready to do battle, the war is over. Choosing your battles with care is a very good idea. Reasonable guidelines help you avoid unnecessary scrimmages that will only exhaust you. For example:

- Craig can wear his hair down to his shoulders as long as it is clean and combed.

- Susan can wear a T-shirt to church as long as there are no references to drugs, bands, violence, profanity, or Satan.

- Aaron can listen to any band he likes, but not to gangsta rap.

These behaviors may still not be what you would like, what you would prefer, but as long as they do no harm, they are harmless. Even if the teenager dresses like a rodeo clown after a rainstorm and listens to music with blasting guitar riffs, screaming incomprehensible lyrics, it is better to let go on these issues than to give on critical issues that do involve your teenager's welfare, safety, or well-being.

Well, what if your teenager's choice does involve his or her welfare, safety, or well-being? For example, should you let your teenager dress like a gangster? Or have contact with adult strangers over the Internet? Or listen to profanity-laced, sexist, and/or racist music? Your teenager could get shot, or sexually assaulted, or have his or her mind polluted. For most parents, this kind of restriction on their teenager's choice comes under the heading of reasonable guidelines. You may need to set limits and veto choices over the limits, but if you do, be prepared to monitor and supervise compliance. It may not be easy. Saying no and meaning it rarely is.

In chapters 3 and 4, I show you how to choose an effective consequence, tie it to the rule, and to enforce it. Rules rule!

CHAPTER THREE
NATURAL AND LOGICAL CONSEQUENCES

There are three kinds of consequences we use in this book: natural, logical, and active. (Active consequences will be covered in chapter 4.)

Natural Consequences

A *natural consequence* is one that happens naturally without the parent having to do anything. It comes about as part of the natural order of things.

- If I spend all of my money on my date, I don't have the gas money to get to work.

- When I don't ask my parent to sign my permission slip in time to go on the camping trip, I stay home.

- If I don't get my clothes in the hamper on washday, I wear my cleanest pair of dirty underwear.

Natural consequences are predictive of the kind of sanctions the adolescent will face as an adult for making illogical or irresponsible choices— as long as you don't step in and rescue him from the effects of the natural consequence. Natural consequences provide good opportunities to learn that when you choose a certain behavior, you're choosing the consequence that goes with it. Natural consequences are very effective learning tools for that reason.

CHAPTER THREE

Logical Consequences

A *logical consequence* is one that is arranged beforehand by someone and is logically related to the misbehavior. The consequence is devised by the parent for the teenager to experience as a result of his behavior choice. The logical consequence works best when it is tied to a *consequence rule*, as you can see in the example below, although it can be devised on the spot if necessary when your teenager engages in an unexpected misbehavior.

- When I use your tools without permission, the tools are locked up until you are satisfied that I can use them, clean them, and put them away properly.

- I am grounded from using the car for two days for not returning it at the specified time.

- If I get a ticket for speeding, I lose the use of the car for a week. If I get a second ticket, I lose the use of the car for a week and then can only drive under direct parental supervision for another week.

- Since I went to a prohibited site on the Internet, I have no computer use for a specified period and then I can use it only under supervision.

- I let a friend talk me into skipping math class, so I get an extra hour of math homework tonight and two extra pages of math problems on the weekend.

Confiscation and Forfeiture

Confiscation and forfeiture are two types of logical consequences. They mean that when a teenager chooses to make an inappropriate choice, he or she pays a price. This involves confiscation or forfeiture of items or services.

- If you leave your skateboard out in the driveway, I'll confiscate it for three days the first time, seven days the second time, and ten days the third.

- If I find your denim jacket on the living room floor again, I'll confiscate it for three to ten days, depending.

• If I find pornography or weapons or drugs, I'll confiscate them permanently.

Confiscation works very well for kids who are forgetful, lazy, or have things that they should not have. Forfeiture can be used to deter insolent or defiant behavior. Take away a possession as a cost. Tell your teenager that you will not play a game of "catch" (back and forth). The first time you need to take away a possession because of insulting or uncooperative behavior, it will be donated to charity.

Make the item small and something that is not personal. Make a "hit list" of such possessions so your teenager will know what to expect if he or she keeps it up. Give away the CD you have bought, a movie pass that was to be given for cooperative behavior, or the weekly allowance. A kid at the homeless shelter will be tickled to get any of these items.

You can also take away routine favors or services you do for your kids, such as driving them to the mall, or permitting them to use the car, your time, or your money. Now they are walking or staying home with empty pockets because they couldn't keep their mouths shut—something to think about.

You want to get your teenager's attention and cooperation and show that you mean business. Confiscation and forfeiture are very effective means of transacting such business.

Overcorrection

Another behavioral technique that can be used as a logical consequence is overcorrection. Your teenager must "practice" a behavior until he or she has it right. Have her put away her bike three or four times in a row. When he yells and has a cursing fit, have him repeat himself until he can speak to you or someone else in a polite and calm manner. Repeat the task until it is done satisfactorily. Most kids hate overcorrection, and many learn to do better the first time.

Community Service

You can't think of an appropriate logical consequence for a certain behavior? Then have your teenager perform a number of hours of community service. Have her "volunteer" for a shift at the soup kitchen. Have him tutor younger children at the community center. Have her pull weeds from the elderly neighbor's garden.

Occasional Misbehavior

Can you use a logical consequence in connection with a misbehavior for which you have no consequence rule in place? Yes, this is for misbehavior that is not an ongoing problem, but rather one that happens once in a blue moon.

- If I break the window, I need to pay restitution and help install a new window

- If I swear at the teacher, I need to make a formal apology.

- If I run away from home for the very first time, I'll be given a small amount of freedom out of the house until I gradually earn back all of my free time.

The key point in using a logical consequence as a discipline tool is that the consequence is most effective when it is tied to a consequence rule, that is, it is set beforehand and is logically related to the misbehavior. Occasionally, misbehavior will happen for the first time or will be so infrequent that you do not need a consequence rule. On these occasions, I advise you to arrange a logical consequence on the spot, as long as it can be logically related to the misbehavior.

Return to the list of problem behaviors you wrote down while reading chapter 2 (page 14). Practice devising a logical consequence for each of the behaviors you listed.

Natural and Logical Consequences at Work

Lee

Lee was hungry. He had missed dinner the night before and now he was ready for a big, hearty breakfast. He had just finished combing his hair just the right way so that it would look cool practically the whole day. By the time Lee got to the breakfast table his mother was picking up the last of the dishes and putting them in the sink. Lee was puzzled.

"Where's mine?" he asked. "Didn't you wait for me?"

"Good morning," his mother said.

"Where's breakfast?" Lee asked again.

"Breakfast is at 6:30," his father announced. "It's now 7:10. Everybody is leaving in five minutes."

"But I didn't get any dinner!" Lee protested. "I was at Ben's house last night, and just now I was doing my hair."

"Uh huh," Lee's mother said. "Dinner is at 6 o'clock. You came in at 7."

"You wouldn't even let me make a lousy sandwich last night."

"And we said that we would see you for breakfast at 6:30," Lee's mother said

"Do you hate me? Think I'm fat? Is this some kind of Korean thing?"

"You'll have to wait till lunch," Lee's father said.

"It's not fair!"

"It's time to go," the father said.

"Would you like a piece of leftover toast and a glass of milk to take with you to the bus stop?" Lee's mother asked.

"No, that would look stupid," Lee replied.

Lee walked heavily out to the bus stop. He could hear his stomach growl as he thought about what mean and unreasonable parents he was stuck with. That evening Lee washed his hands and helped set the table. He smiled broadly when dinner began at 6 o'clock.

Vicky

Vicky had worked hard on mowing the lawn and trimming the bushes. This chore was above and beyond her regular routine of chores and she was doing it to earn some extra money from her parents. They had agreed to pay the minimum wage. Now she was anxious to collect her $12.00 and to go shopping. She was surprised when her mother handed her a ten-dollar bill.

"Uh, Mom, it's actually $12.00. That's how long I worked."

"I know it's $12.00, dear. I subtracted $2.00 for the maid service."

"Excuse me?"

"For the maid service. Today is washday."

"We don't have a maid, Mom."

"That's right. Do you remember that I told everyone in the family that I was going to charge $1.00 for every article of clothing I found lying on your bedroom floor on washday?"

"Okay, Mom. I get the point. Can I have my $2.00 now?"

"Not this time, Vicky. If you want maid service you have to pay for it. It's only logical, don't you think?"

The next washday Vicky scoured her bedroom for any clothes that had been left on the floor—or anywhere else—and dropped them into the hamper. She thought it quite amusing when her brother was charged $3.00 for two socks and a pair of underwear.

Steve

Steve was a little worried about the traffic ticket. He'd only had his driver's license a month, and this was already his second ticket. The cops were out to get teenage drivers, that's all. Everybody else was going that fast. Steve knew that his dad would go ballistic and yell and scream, but after that was over he'd tell him to be "a hell of a lot more careful" and then would pay the fine for him. It wouldn't be too bad.

"Dad? I got another stupid traffic ticket. Can you take care of it?"

"What was the ticket for?"

"Oh, speeding. You know how cops lie in wait for you."

"Were you speeding?"

Steve hesitated before answering. He was a little puzzled. This was usually when his dad started swearing and yelling. Steve's dad looked at him with a calm expression. He had completed a "decisive parenting" course at the high school just three days before.

"Well, yeah, sort of," Steve answered finally.

"Do you remember that we established a consequence rule about driving?"

"Yeah."

"What is the rule?"

"I don't know, something about following traffic laws."

"The rule is obey all of the traffic laws."

"Okay, so?"

"And what is the consequence that goes with the rule?"

"Dad, come on. . . ."

"That you'll pay all of your own traffic fines, and that you'll lose the use of the car for two weeks for every traffic fine you receive."

"Come on, Dad. You can't be serious about that stuff."

"The alternative is that you'll pay your own fine and either your mother or I will ride along with you when you use the car for two weeks. Paying your own fine is the natural result of getting a ticket, and losing the right to drive is only logical. Which of the driving options would you prefer?"

"I don't have any money! You've always paid for stuff before."

"That's okay, we can find some jobs for you to do. Do you want us to ride along or do you want to lose the car keys for two weeks?"

"Ride along. At least I can still drive. But do I really have to work?"

"Son, welcome to the real world."

Steve shoveled snow from all of his neighbor's walks. He cleaned out the garage and refinished his mother's oak dresser. In two weeks' time he had enough money to pay his traffic fine. For two weeks his parents rode along whenever Steve wanted to use the car. After the two weeks were over, Steve didn't drive over the speed limit even when his friends urged him to do so. He didn't get another speeding ticket for nine years. This occurred when his wife was in labor and he was rushing her to the hospital for the birth of his first child.

CHAPTER FOUR
ACTIVE CONSEQUENCES FOR CHALLENGING SITUATIONS

All adolescents at some time defy their parents. Remember when your teenager was two and her favorite words were "no" and "mine"? Much the same mentality will apply from time to time now that your teenager is older. Periods of rebelliousness are normal and to be expected.

Defiant-Behaving Teenagers

Most kids resist consequences at least some of the time, but what about the teenager who doesn't respond consistently to discipline through consequences most of the time? This is not a *bad* kid; this is a *defiant-behaving* kid. Defiant-behaving teenagers defy rules and adult authority almost without fail. If this is your teenager, you need a unique set of parenting skills to change his or her behavior. This chapter and the next will teach you these skills.

Common defiant, irresponsible behaviors look like these:

- Eli says "So?" or "I don't care" when you lay out the consequence for his misbehavior. Take away his Game Boy for a week? "Go ahead—keep it; I don't want the stupid thing anyway."

- Julia resists discipline by pretending that rules and consequences don't apply to her. She is special. She is above that sort of thing. When consequences for misbehavior do come, she is incredulous that you are so blind and brainless, that you don't understand rules only apply to lesser mortals and certainly not to her. "I'm thirteen. I can do what I want, see?"

- Alex tells you to take your list of rules and consequences, fold 'em four ways, and stick 'em where the sun don't shine; he reacts with open hostility and rebellion to parental discipline; he uses threats and violence with his parents: "I wouldn't try to stop me if I were you."

- Paul engages in unacceptable behavior habitually: he wants to use your wallet as an ATM machine, sees nothing wrong with turning his bedroom into a hot-sheet hotel, and thinks that drinking and driving is an acquired skill. To top it off, a kid like Paul will try to minimize his involvement in wrongdoing. After all, he put the fire out, he returned the car after a week, and he only kicked the guy in the head once.

- Elizabeth abhors taking responsibility for her behavior. It's the other kid's fault. It was circumstances beyond her control. She wanted to do the right thing, but people and circumstances forced her to do the wrong thing.

Teenagers who engage in these kinds of behaviors typically lack two things: insight into the reasons for their behavior and empathy for those whom it affects. When asked, "Why did you do this?" a common answer is "I don't know. I just did." As they frequently act on impulse and emotion, they often cannot give you a logical explanation for why they engaged in some particular misbehavior. "I don't know. I just did" is therefore a truthful response. Setting up a logical consequence beforehand for the teenager to experience fails to change behavior because these kids often don't think ahead.

The same is likely to be true with their ability to learn from the natural consequence. These teenagers are not considering the consequences and the ramifications of their behavior for the next day or next week. They are concerned with doing what they want to do, when they want to do it, and the hell with you or anybody else that gets in their way. After it happens is when they first think about the resulting pregnancy, injury, addiction, expulsion, or criminal charges.

In addition, because their wants and wishes come first, these teenagers often hurt other people. Just as these kids lack insight into why they do what they do, it is hard for them to consider what might be the effect of their actions on others. They are not thinking about the possible trouble and misery for their parents and other people. Some kids have such weak attachments with parents and others that they also *don't care* about the effects of their behavior. Since the more common natural and logical consequences often do not work very well or for very long with these adolescents, what can you do instead?

The Active Consequence

What works consistently well with the teenager whose behavior is so defiant or irresponsible is the active consequence. This type of consequence restricts the teenager's *freedom*. The active consequence is a freedom-restricting consequence brought on by your *teenager's choice*—she chooses to have you involved by virtue of the poor choices she makes. You take over making good choices for your teenager until she proves able to do so. *You take a very active role, sometimes long-term, in fulfilling the consequences you or others apply to your teenager's behavior.*

Parents should consider using active consequences when they *know* their teenager has a consistent history of defiant behavior. For example, if you feel your teenager's friends are less than desirable and you restrict your teenager from seeing them without just cause, contact with those friends will automatically become more desirable in your teenager's mind. His friend is now forbidden fruit and becomes an object of considerable want and need.

If, on the other hand, you have evidence of repeated shoplifting or some other irresponsible behavior when with this friend, you have just cause to closely monitor and supervise the contacts with her friend, or restrict access to the friend. Until when? Until your teenager demonstrates by her behavior that she has become trustworthy. *Active parental involvement* is the essence of the active consequence, as compared to no involvement whatsoever in natural consequences and no involvement beyond devising the consequence in logical consequences.

Any teenager whose behavior is habitually defiant or irresponsible can be moved to a position of assuming personal responsibility for his or her behavior with time, commitment, and the diligent application of a sound discipline and behavior change plan on your part. Using active consequences you can and you will have good success.

How to Set the Active Consequence into Motion

The active consequence consists of physical action and mental attentiveness on the parent's part. You will use any or all of these actions (active consequences) to ensure compliance on your teenager's part:

- Intercession

- Networking

- Tracking

- Monitoring

- Supervision

Your intention in using these five skills is to form an open hand, not a clenched fist. Like natural and logical consequences, the active consequence is designed to help, not to hammer, to provide the opportunity to teach and to learn. It is your tool of choice when the other two kinds of consequences don't do the job.

Intercession

Intercession involves being an active mentor to your teenager, or finding help related to altering his or her problem behavior. Sometimes, our most effective action is to step back and ask others to step forward. There may be times when you need someone else to dig at the roots of your teenager's problem behavior, rather than trying to trim back the branches.

The teenager may be consistently misbehaving in some part because he has a psychological or medical condition and won't be able to change his behavior until that problem is addressed. The teenager may need to see a psychotherapist to talk through his problems and learn some new skills. He may have a medical condition that requires medication to help alter his behavior. He may need to see a physician, an optometrist, or an audiologist in order to feel better or to see or hear better.

Early Warning Signs of Problem Behavior

These are early behavioral signs that your teenager may be heading for trouble. Any one of these signs alone may not be enough to indicate a problem. But when you see several together and in a consistent pattern, you should follow up. Talk to your teenager and tell him or her what you have seen. If that is not successful, you may want to talk to a competent family therapist or mental health therapist who can help you and your teenager sort things out. The professional can make recommendations about what should happen next. The behavior to look for includes the following:

- Loss of interest in school: skipping, incomplete assignments, failing grades
- Loss of interest in usual activities: hobbies, clubs, sports, time with family
- Loss of interest in friends: not returning phone calls, not going out with friends, not dating, friends not contacting the teenager
- New friends your teenager doesn't want you to meet
- Becoming secretive or lying to parents about whereabouts and activities; having large sums of money or unexplained gifts
- Refusing to discuss with parents or other adults what's happening in their lives
- Increased interest in things that are overly antisocial, such as some kinds of violent movies, music, and games; worrisome clothing or hair styles, jewelry, body art, language, and gestures; putting up offensive wall posters or reading offensive materials
- Significant changes in mood and/or physical appearance, sleeping, and eating habits, and ability to concentrate on everyday activities; being "sick" more often than usual; unusual weight loss

None of these signs *alone* necessarily indicates a serious or consistent problem. Your teenager may be merely trying a new image, and some of the things may be a matter of personal taste and preference that can be handled under the heading of your reasonable guidelines (page 18).

A consistent pattern of several of these behaviors occurring together over a period of time, however, may indicate a serious problem is about to arrive or is already here.

Some kids are addicted to drugs and/or alcohol and need immediate assessment and treatment. This may mean outpatient or specialized long-term care in a hospital or treatment facility. A number of rebellious or troubled kids become actively suicidal or self-abusive. Such self-abuse, too, requires immediate specialized assessment and intercession on your teenager's behalf.

You can also be an active intercessor for your teenager in other areas. You can actively cultivate a relationship with your "difficult" child by practicing the communication and problem-solving skills presented in later chapters of this book and by showing your love in active ways. You can also note that, in fact, your teenager could be acting out family stress and dysfunction. In this case, your family may need the beneficial intercession of family therapy.

Further, some kids are enmeshed with delinquent friends or associates and need specialized intervention to leave the lifestyle behind.

Sometimes your teenager needs academic help. Many kids become rebellious about attending school and doing homework because their academic self-esteem has been beaten down by a sense of failure and rejection. Many kids with irresponsible behavior have learning disabilities that have not been identified or appropriately dealt with through their school years. Interceding by providing tutoring help and remedial work can be a tremendous benefit for such kids. Further, many schools now have adult mentor volunteers to assist kids who need help. Accessing available help is active intervention for your child.

Networking

Networking means gathering and sharing information with the places and people your teenager is involved with on a daily or frequent basis, such as the school, job site, clubs, religious center, or agencies. It may also include sharing information with family members, other kids who know your teenager, and especially with his or her friends' parents. You want adults in your network who know your child, who work with your child, or who love your child.

Does networking mean you're going to share intimate details about your teenager's life with anyone who asks? Certainly not. Does it mean you're going to be gathering and disseminating certain information about the teenager? On a *need-to-know basis*, yes. For example, are you going to tell her friends that she was molested? No. Would you tell her therapist that? Yes. It is information that could help account for her behavior. Would you tell her teachers about the rules that you have for her completing and turning in her homework? Yes. It is information that is relevant for the teachers to know.

If you know and trust your teenager's principal, teachers and school counselor, coaches, work supervisor, youth pastor, juvenile probation officer (if she has one), and your teenager's friends' parents, then you can share and gather information that will be consistently useful to you in helping your teenager. The same may be true for adults in your neighborhood, who may know your teenager less well, but have information about the teenager's behavior that you'll want to know. You may also want family members in your network—grandparents, aunts, uncles, cousins, and others—who can share what they see and know in regard to your teenager's behavior.

- If my drug-abusing son comes to work stoned, I want to know that.

- If my daughter, who is a habitual thief, comes to school wearing a new leather jacket she "found behind the gym," I want to hear about it.

- If my youngest son, who likes to hit people, is seen assaulting another child in the hallway, please call me at once.

Is that asking people to spy and snitch on my child? No, that's asking people to report what they see, letting me make the decision about whether the information is important or not. Further, you're providing information about what you know so there is mutual sharing. If you think your teenager is involved in a gang—or is a "wannabe" gang member—ask the network to look for signs and activity. Any teenager who is skipping school, running away, using drugs, or engaged in criminal activity will have a much harder time doing so when his or her parents have the support of a personal network helping you look over the kid's shoulder.

When seeking to establish your network, you gain an awareness of what the other adults in your teenager's life are like. What are their values and what kind of standards for behavior he or she is likely to observe while your teenager is present. When you ask people to network you may not always get a positive response. Some adults will not share information with you. Some may give you false information. You may choose not to include particular adults in your network because in your experience they are untrustworthy. Some adults may even attempt to sabotage your discipline. However, most adults will welcome your interest and involvement. They don't want to deal with a misbehaving teenager any more than you do, but will do so when they believe that corrective action will be taken.

Networking is a useful tool in preventing misbehavior. It can also be a useful tool in establishing positive behavior. Think about all the adults in your teenager's life who can exert influence and model positive behavior. Are there adults of good will who can mentor and model success in life for your teenager? Ask these people to spend time with your teenager—to encourage and to lift him or her up to the higher places. Teenagers usually respond very well to adults outside their families who take a genuine and healthy interest in them.

Networking Worksheet

To use the skill of networking with the adults in your teenager's life, you'll need to contact them by phone (or preferably in person). You'll want to explain to them that you're working on helping your teenager gain compliance in a particular area (or areas) and would like to enlist their support. Here is a sample script you may want to use.

1. "Hello, I am _____'s mother (father). I am calling because I want to have contact with the adults in _____'s life. Since you are my child's teacher (or friend's parent, counselor, school

nurse, employer, coach, probation officer, youth pastor, etc.), I wanted to get to know you."

2. "I want to take a moment to introduce myself and to let you know a few of the rules I/we have for my child since he (she) will be in contact with you."

3. State several of your rules. You may want to explain briefly why you have the consequence rule.

4. Ask for the adult's support. You may ask him or her to contact you if he or she believes one of the rules has been violated. "You can call or e-mail me/us at . . . ; home/cell phone numbers are . . . ; these are my/our work hours, and here is how I/we can be contacted at work. . . ."

5. If this is a friend's parent, you may want to add, "I'd like to know some of the rules that you have for your child so that I can monitor and support those rules when the kids are with me."

Network Chain

You can also establish a network chain of concerned adults. Parents and teachers agree to post information for one another on the Internet or through cell phone trees. At times there will be false rumors and fabrications, but the vigilant parent can verify tips about unsupervised parties, adults who harbor runaways, planned fights after school, and other tidbits that the kids may not want you to know.

Parents who live in high crime areas have also banded together to form neighborhood "kid" watches. These parents share what they know about gang, drug, and other criminal activity that might involve their teenagers and agree to help each other.

Network Meeting

Some parents periodically organize informal networking meetings. For example, at the beginning of the school year, a parent calls a networking meeting of her daughter's school counselor, work supervisor, and the teenager's best friend's parents for a short get-together over coffee.

Kids, Gangs, Cults, and Negative Peers

Most parents say that kids who get involved with gangs, cults, and negative peers are kids who are generally noncompliant and out of control. Actually, it has been my experience that most of these kids are *very compliant*. They are compliant with what is demanded of them to be members of the gang, cult, or group.

What do you get when you become a member of such a group? You have a name and an identity. You are expected to adhere to certain strongly held beliefs that are an integral part of the group, and to accept the group's moral values. You have definite rules for your behavior, and usually there are strong consequences for not following the rules. You're given love and companionship. You have someone to talk to who will listen to your side of things and give you guidance as to what you should do. And you have someone who will support you and back you up in times of trouble. In other words, you have a family.

By joining this "family," you'll receive structure and support, coupled with freedom and limits, the very things the teenager receives from the authoritative parent, the kind this book is teaching you how to be. The difference is that what the group offers goes in a negative direction and what you offer goes in a positive direction.

So how do you keep your teenager from joining gangs, cults, or other negative peer groups? You give your child consistently the things he or she could get from these other sources: *strong attachments and strong behavioral controls*. Adolescents especially need the left hand of strong attachments and the right hand of strong behavioral controls. Kids are considerably less likely to be involved with negative groups and peers when they are consistently and positively involved with their families. They cannot do both. Home is where the heart is when there is a heart in the home.

Because the teenager has a history of performing poorly in school with frequent truancy, a plan for academic success is discussed. The school counselor agrees to help implement the plan with the teachers. The work supervisor agrees to support the plan by tying the number of hours the teenager can work to how well she is doing academically. The best friend's parents agree to limit the amount of time the kids can be together and spend in their home if the teenager has homework to do. They will also have the house monitored by neighbors to make certain that the kids don't spend the school day hanging out there.

The result of establishing these networks is parents who have moved up their chances of having success in implementing their rules, and who feel supported and encouraged in their parenting. By networking, parents no longer must "go it alone."

Tracking

People leave behind evidence of their behavior. If you're not sure if your teenager is engaged in a particular problem behavior, look for the tracks—the physical evidence—that could lead you to the answer.

- If you think your son is using drugs, and you have more than casual suspicion, you may search his room, car, backpack, and clothes looking for paraphernalia or the drugs themselves. You may ask the school to search his locker. You may look in his eyes and smell his breath. You'll watch his behavior and monitor his mood. You may take him to a clinic for a urinalysis for drugs, or send a hair sample to a lab. And when you find drugs you may call the police and have the teenager criminally charged, or seek out a drug rehabilitation program.

- Your daughter is failing all of her classes. You can track her daily academic progress with the Daily Class Assignment Report, coupled with tutoring and networking with her teachers.

- Your youngest son has difficulty not shoplifting at the mall. You'll track what items he brings into the house, and demand to see a receipt for each one. If he does not have a receipt, the item goes back to the store or is donated to charity.

Monitoring

Closely related to tracking is the skill of monitoring. Monitoring means reviewing the teenager's behavior choices and then following up as needed.

- If you think your daughter is not telling the truth about her whereabouts—she said that she went to the library to study, but you have reason to believe she may be at a party that she did not have permission to go to—you'll call the library to verify or go and meet her at the location of the party.

- If your younger daughter often skips her biology class, and you've networked with her teacher and school to get a call at work when she does skip, you will go to school and escort her to each class the next day.

- Did the kids clean their room? You'll go in and find out.

- Were there any problems when your son stayed overnight at the Jones's house? You'll call the Jones parents and find out.

- Did she lie about Marcie giving her the sweater? You'll check it out with Marcie.

Monitoring allows you to gather the evidence that things are going well or that they are not. A teenager is considerably less likely to lie or attempt to cover up misbehavior when his or her parent is monitoring consistently.

Supervision

Supervision is a more stringent form of monitoring. It means you need to be there both physically and psychologically for the teenager to ensure compliance.

- You'll stand in the doorway while he cleans his room.

- You'll keep an eye on the clock to ensure that she observes the phone time limit rule.

- You'll ride the school bus or sit in class with her because she can't make mature and appropriate decisions for herself when she is alone.

- You'll have him empty his pockets outside the mall before you take him home.

Preventative Supervision

There is also a type of supervision I call "preventive" because you take physical action to head off misbehavior.

- The teenager who habitually shoplifts doesn't shop in stores unless he is under the eyeball supervision of a responsible adult.

- The teenager who cannot be trusted not to make long-distance phone calls without permission finds a phone lock.

- The teenager who eats dessert before dinner finds the dessert locked in the pantry.

- The teenager who likes to rummage through her parents' bedroom looking for "spare change" finds the bedroom door locked.

- The teenager who refuses to get out of bed in the morning finds a parent dislodging her from the bed.

This type of discipline is especially effective because it is much easier to *keep* a kid out of trouble in the first place than it is to *get* a kid out of trouble after the fact.

How much will most teenagers like and appreciate their parents doing these things? About as well as when they were forced to take baths, pick up their toys, and eat their vegetables when they were younger; in other words, not in the least. Which is perfectly okay. Most parents are not going to be too wild about needing to do discipline in this way either. The trick for the teenager is to get Mom and Dad to lay off by doing what he or she needs to do the first time, and eventually, without having to be asked.

But aren't active consequences intrusive and likely to make a rebellious kid just that more rebellious? And doesn't their use serve to erode trust between the parent and teenager? After all, we don't want to become dictators and have the kids hate us.

Active consequences are designed to be intrusive. Like all manners of discipline, they are meant to be unpleasant and at times embarrassing for the recipient. They teach the child to cultivate the habit of *think before you act, plan before you do*. Think about the consequence that goes with behavior you choose and then plan ahead.

Active consequences can also help stop the rebellious teenager dead in her tracks by denying her the *opportunity* to misbehave. If you need to use active consequences frequently, it probably means there is very little trust between you and your teenager already. As your teenager learns to comply with rules and expectations, she is building trust between the two of you.

Escalating Levels of Consequences

Consequence Rule
Rule: Put all dirty clothes in the laundry hamper before washday.

Consequence: Clothes that are not in the hamper will not be washed.

1. Natural Consequence: Something that happens naturally without parental action.

   "If I don't put my dirty clothes in the hamper on wash day, I will have to wear my cleanest pair of dirty underwear."

2. Logical Consequence: Something arranged beforehand and logically connected to the misbehavior.

   "If I don't get my clothes in the hamper on wash day, I will have to do my own laundry."

3. Active Consequence: Something arranged beforehand and attended to in person by someone in authority.

   "If I don't get my clothes in the hamper on wash day, my dad will escort me to my bedroom and hang around until I have picked up all of my dirty clothes, and put them in the hamper." (Tool used: preventative supervision)

That is why active consequences are so effective when less intrusive forms of discipline are not.

Your teenager may "hate" you for a time, but that is preferable to his feeling contempt because you cannot influence or control his behavior. The point is not so much whether the active consequence is liked and appreciated, as whether it is effective and gets a response. Indeed it is and it does.

Earning Freedom

So how does a teenager get a parent to back off and stop employing these embarrassing and annoying, and, from some teenagers' perspectives, totally unjust active consequences? How does a parent get a teenager to grow beyond needing active consequences? The answer is simple: by having your child become consistently compliant with the consequence rules and by exercising the freedom that comes with it.

Most teenagers crave one thing more than anything else: *freedom.* They want the freedom to make decisions about the things that affect their lives. They will often tell you that when attempting to strike a deal to do something that they want to do: "Look, you let me do this and I'll have a chance to show you that I am responsible and trustworthy." The formula looks like this: freedom—responsibility—trust. The problem with this preferred formula is that the parent gives the incentive first (freedom), followed by the accountability factor (responsibility), followed by the dependability factor (trust).

With responsible kids the formula works just fine. When given the freedom to make their own choices, they assume the responsibility willingly and well. This naturally builds a trust bond between the parent and child. The result is that we can extend even more freedom to the adolescent. With the semi-responsible and irresponsible teenager we'll have a problem putting the formula into effect.

The semi-responsible teenager will consistently have difficulty handling her freedom in one or two areas of concern. She does her chores and homework consistently. She attends school regularly. But she is stealing money and alcohol from the house and giving it to and using it with her boyfriend. When asked, she has lied about it.

The irresponsible teenager has difficulty handling her freedom in most areas of concern. She does her chores or homework only when she is prodded into doing them, and then she does the bare minimum. She skips school regularly. She consistently steals money and alcohol from the house, which she shares with her boyfriend and peers, and when asked, routinely lies about it.

With semi-responsible and irresponsible kids like these, the formula works better this way: trust—responsibility—freedom. The teenager earns trust by becoming consistently compliant with rules and expectations. She demonstrates responsibility by accepting the consequences that go with the rules. She demonstrates responsibility by being consistently trustworthy in little things too: doing her chores and homework without having to be pushed or prodded, getting to bed on time, getting up in the morning, being home at the proper time, and not arguing or being deliberately irritating. She earns freedom by demonstrating that she can handle the freedom she is given.

By doing these things consistently, your teenager is taking the initiative to be responsible. She is rightly earning freedom—a small amount of freedom at first, with increasingly more freedom as she demonstrates more responsible and trustworthy behavior.

Many kids have a good deal of personal freedom. They can come and go, do things with their friends, do their homework and chores when they choose to, have special privileges, and make most of their own decisions. These teenagers needed to earn their freedom, based upon their demonstrated level of trustworthy and responsible behavior. They don't have total freedom—no one does—and their parents are aware of what is happening in their lives and the decisions they are making. This is the kind of freedom that families should strive for.

When the wanted behavior is consistently in place, discontinue using the consequence. It may require a one-time use of the consequence—be it the natural, logical, or active consequence—or it may take months of consistent use, but the end will come. Afterward, continue to use positive rewards to reinforce the occurrence of the new positive behavior.

Through your use of consequences—negative consequences for misbehavior, and positive consequences for positive behavior—your teenager is in a position to get what he wants—and not just from you, but from other adult authority figures as well. How? By demonstrating that he is trustworthy with the freedom he does have. The more trustworthy he is, the more freedom he has; the less trustworthy, the less freedom.

Tell your teenager, "You get just as much freedom as you demonstrate that you can handle successfully." Is this not the same standard you used when your child was younger? When did you decide that he no longer needed a babysitter? When could she go to the park, or stay overnight at a friend's house, or even go on her first date? For most parents, it was when their children demonstrated by the yardstick of their behavior that they could handle the situation.

In complying with consequence rules, *teenagers* control the amount, degree, and kind of freedom that they earn in the discipline plan. You can wait for kids to learn to "be more responsible," or you can now place the weight of their personal accountability squarely on their own shoulders.

- You can choose any elective course you like—you just can't choose to fail.

- You can consume any healthy substance you like—but not illegal drugs.

- You can stay out as long as you like—as long as you're home before curfew.

What do you have when you have a teenager who consistently makes the choice to pass all of his classes, and not use illegal drugs, and be home by curfew? A kid who has a great deal more personal freedom that he otherwise would have based upon his behavior; a teenager who is moving toward becoming a self-directed and self-motivated person who requires very little active parental discipline. That is exactly what we want.

Active Consequences Needed

Julie

Julie was still in bed when her mother called her for the fourth time. She had been out late with her boyfriend the night before and both of them had gotten pretty smashed. Julie was tired and had absolutely no intention of going to school today. Her mother was just as adamant that Julie would get out of bed and go to school.

"Julie! I'm going to be late for work. Now come on, honey, get out of bed. If you're late for school one more time you'll get suspended."

Julie pulled the blanket under her chin.

"Julie!"

"What!?"

"You know what. Get out of bed right now."

"I'm sick."

"You're not sick. You're hung over."

"I wasn't drinking," Julie lied. "And I'm not going to school today."

"Jew-lee!" her mother whined. "You want to fail all of your classes again?"

"Oh, so I'm going to fail? I'm just a total failure."

"I didn't say that."

"But that's what you meant."

"What I'm I going to do with you? Julie, I love you. But if you don't stop drinking and using drugs—"

"Oh, so now I'm a drug addict."

"No. . . . It's that boyfriend of yours. Todd gets you to do—"

"Oh, so now I'm a whore!"

"Julie. . . . Fine. You do what you want today. Just please go to school tomorrow."

"I will. Just quit worrying about me, okay. Everything is fine."

"Okay, just don't be mad. Okay?"

"I'm not, Mom. Love you."

"Love you, too, honey."

Julie's mother left for work confident that she had gotten through to Julie about the importance of regular school attendance. Julie went back to sleep and slept most of the day. That evening she went out drinking with Todd. She did not attend school the rest of the week and was suspended. At the end of the month when Julie missed her period, it was confirmed that she was pregnant.

David

David was happy. He'd gotten his share of the money for the car stereos and now he could go to the concert Friday night. He didn't really like the idea of stealing car stereos, but hey, if people were dumb enough to have them, then they ought to lose them. At least that was the way Jesse explained it. Jesse was twenty-three years old, had done "hard" time, and was a member of the Aryan Brotherhood. He knew what he was talking about. He'd seen life and stuff. Jesse had told David about how Jews and other minority groups were set to take over the world. David didn't like that idea one bit. David was putting his money away when his dad walked through the front door.

> "Hi, guy."
> "Hey Dad."

David's father was exhausted after an eleven-hour workday. He was looking at another one just like it tomorrow.

> "You want to eat out?"
> "Mom's not home yet," David said.
> "She won't be for another hour. She said go ahead."
> "Let's do it."
> "You got all your chores done?"
> "Yeah."
> "School work?"
> "Yeah"
> "Anything new?"
> "Nope."
> "Cool. Let's do the steak place."

David's father left the house with David that evening feeling assured that he knew everything of importance that was happening in his son's life. David was glad that evening that he had such good parents. All such goodwill evaporated the following week when David was arrested for burglary and theft. His father was puzzled when he found a racist comic book and a swastika armband in David's bedroom closet.

Leah

Leah was talking on the phone to her friend when her grandmother came into the living room.

> "Leah, get off the phone."
> "What?"

"You said you'd pick up the living room an hour ago, and you're still talking. Come on, girl."

Leah's grandmother began to pick up the clothes on the floor.

"I'll call you back," Leah said to her friend and hung up. "Jeez, Grandma, that's embarrassing when I'm on the phone like that."

Leah's grandmother began to stack the newspapers.

"Come and help me," she said.

Leah moved empty soda cans from one end of the couch to the other.

"Have you feed Lucky yet?"

"Not yet. You told me to clean up the living room. I've been doing my homework."

Leah pointed to the undisturbed pile of books next to the couch.

"She's your dog, you know." Leah's grandmother said.

Leah's grandmother got out the vacuum cleaner and began to sweep. Leah picked up three empty soda cans and slowly walked in to the kitchen. She dropped the cans into the recycling bin and then walked extra slowly back into the living room. Her grandmother was rewinding the cord on the vacuum cleaner.

"There," she said brightly. "Now that wasn't so bad."

Leah agreed that it wasn't so bad. She picked up the phone to call her friend. The homework was never done that evening because Leah "didn't have time." She took an F on her assignment. The dog was not fed until late that night when Leah's grandmother got tired of listening to the animal howl.

Active Consequences at Work

Julie

Julie's mother called the county health department and arranged to have Julie undergo a drug/alcohol abuse assessment. It was determined that Julie was in the early stages of dependency. Julie was subsequently enrolled against her will in an adolescent drug treatment and wilderness experience program. She attempted to escape twice in order to be with

Todd. Julie finally decided, for her baby's sake, and to get out so that she could be with Todd, that she would play the game.

Julie made substantial progress in treatment, but anticipated going home and resuming her customary routine. Julie went home to a different world. Her mother established consequence rules and set consequences for Julie's behavior. Julie was expected to do daily household chores. Because she was so far behind in academic credits, she was enrolled in an alternative high school. Her mother networked with her teachers and counselor and received daily reports on her progress. At night, Julie's mother sat at the kitchen table with her while she did her homework; she supervised her chore completion, and she closely monitored where Julie was, whom she was with, and what she was doing.

At first, Julie fought against these restrictions. But within three weeks her mother's consistency began to pay off and Julie became much more compliant. Julie and her mother began to enjoy each other's company again. Julie received regular prenatal care during her pregnancy. She underwent random urinalysis to detect drug use. She saw a therapist twice a week. She attended AA meetings.

However, Julie still tried to see Todd whenever she could. Todd complained that Julie's mother had called his probation officer, who obtained a court order that he was not to see Julie. Todd wanted Julie to drink and do drugs with him. She said that she would not, for fear of what it might do to the baby. Todd said that if Julie really loved him, she would. When she refused on their third meeting to use drugs, Todd slapped Julie, hard. With the help of her therapist, Julie worked up the courage to call the police. Todd was arrested for assault. He never saw Julie again.

Julie graduated with a GED, gave birth to a healthy baby girl, and is attending a community college studying computer repair. She is clean and sober and attends AA meetings. She lives with her mother and they often laugh together.

David

David was lodged in juvenile hall for six days. He was then given a suspended commitment to a youth detention center by the juvenile court judge. Jesse was arrested and sent back to prison. David was ordered to pay restitution to his victims and to perform a certain number of hours of community service. He was also ordered to attend an education program about gangs and cults. All of David's hate literature and swastikas were burned. David was on probation for nine months. David's parents were required by the court to complete a parenting course. After the course, David's parents arranged to have him enrolled in a community center's after-school program, where he was under constant supervision. On evenings and weekends David's parents required that he inform them where he was going, whom he intended to be with, and what he intended to do. They did spot checks. They required David to bring all of his friends to the house so they could meet them and their parents, and they networked with all of the adults in David's life to get regular reports about his behavior. When David "tested" the rules and expectations, they followed through consistently with set consequences.

As David demonstrated increasingly more trustworthy behavior his parents frequently praised his efforts and restored more of his freedom. They began to allow David to once again make more of his own choices. David did not get into any more difficulty with the law.

Leah

Leah's grandmother insisted that they establish some consequence rules for Leah's problem behaviors. At first Leah refused to participate in rule construction. Leah's grandmother said that she would proceed without her. When Leah saw the first draft of the rules and consequences, she decided that they were too harsh and punitive and then eagerly joined in the second round of rule construction.

Leah was put on a daily schedule for chore and homework completion. Leah's grandmother set up a point chart for Leah to earn positive consequences and freedom in exchange for doing chores and homework to a high standard. Leah's grandmother monitored consistently and did not help her do her work. After a slow start, and within three weeks, Leah was doing her homework and chores about 60 percent of the time without her grandmother's prodding. Within six weeks Leah was doing all of her homework and chores every day with no reminders. Her grades shot up and she and her grandmother found that each had more quality free time to do as they pleased.

CHAPTER FIVE
LEVEL SYSTEMS, POINT ECONOMIES, AND CONTRACTS

The two most common discipline practices parents use with adolescents are grounding and taking away privileges. If these discipline methods work consistently for you, well and good. If they do not—your teenager makes your life miserable for the two weeks he is off his privileges and in the house—you may need more skills to choose from.

Three skills commonly used in effective juvenile programs that can be adapted to home use are:

- Level Systems—the teenager earns privileges and freedom at different behavior levels

- Point Economies—the teenager earns points that he can exchange for privileges and desires

- Contracts—the teenager and parent make voluntary formal agreements

Use of these skills requires the same level of active parental involvement as the active consequences covered in chapter 4. Likewise, they are extremely effective with *all* teenagers, but can be especially useful with difficult teenagers. You can also use all three skills simultaneously depending on the issue at hand.

Level Systems

In most successful juvenile programs, there is a behavioral level system in place. Teenagers generally start out with a low level of freedom and privilege and work their way up through the system to a maximum level of privileges and freedom.

Something akin to this system can be used at home as an *alternative* to grounding and taking away privileges. Level systems do not work well all the time. However, for serious instances of misbehavior, you may want to give them a try.

When your teenager has engaged in some serious misbehavior, such as running away for days or bringing home all failing grades with multiple incidents of truancy, and you wish to ground him for a time, consider using a level system such as the one illustrated below. (This work is based partly on a level system as developed by psychologists J. Douglas Meyers and George Howard.)

Level I, Forty-Eight Hours

House restriction for forty-eight hours. _____ must stay in the house (unless attending school). There are no privileges at this level. _____ may not talk on the phone, watch TV, play the radio or stereo, use the computer for other than schoolwork, play video games, or have contact with friends. _____ will complete all school assignments and assigned chores without complaint and with parental verification. _____ will not argue or complain about freedom restrictions.

Forty-eight hours of compliant behavior will result in a move to level II status, at the parent's discretion.

Level II, Forty-Eight Hours

Must stay in the house or on the immediate property (unless attending school). Can watch TV and make one fifteen-minute phone call per day. _____ can participate in family outings as long as at least one of the parents is present. _____ will complete all school assignments and assigned chores without complaint and with parental verification.

Forty-eight hours of compliant behavior will result in a move to level III status, at the parent's discretion.

Level III, Twenty-Four Hours

_____ has all of the privileges of level II. In addition, _____ can visit a friend or have a friend visit the house for one hour with parental permission. Further, _____ can watch TV, talk on the phone, play the radio or stereo, play video games, or use the computer to whatever level parents feel is appropriate. _____ will complete all school assignments and assigned chores with parental verification.

Twenty-four hours of compliant behavior will result in a move to level IV status, at the parent's discretion.

Level IV, Twenty-Four Hours

_____ has all of the privileges of level III. _____ can leave the house with parental permission for a specified period of time for an approved activity with a required phone call when he/she arrives at destination. At level IV, parents may require a formal problem-solving meeting with _____ in order to come to agreements about how to prevent a recurrence of the problem behavior that led to the use of the level system.

Twenty-four hours of compliant behavior will result in the removal of the level system restrictions.

Any of the following behaviors will result in a drop in level status as follows:

Verbal abuse: Level I for twenty-four hours.

Physical threats or abuse: Level I for forty-eight hours.

Lying: Level I for twenty-four hours.

Stealing: Level decreased to former level for twenty-four hours plus any legal sanctions.

School behavior problems: Level decreased to former level for twenty-four hours plus school/parent contact with any needed action.

Drug or alcohol use: Level I for seven days plus any needed treatment follow-up.

Persistent negative attitude and behavior: Drop to the former level.

Running away or being gone without permission: Three hours of level I for every hour gone without permission.

Other: To be arranged.

This six-day level system is usually more effective and consistent than a typical grounding. In conventional restrictions, a teenager must only "be there" and "do time" in order to get off grounding. She need not demonstrate any change in behavior or outlook. There are no expectations for trustworthy, responsible behavior, and no method to measure it.

In a level system, the *child* controls the degree of freedom and privilege she receives. She must demonstrate she is trustworthy and responsible with the personal freedom she does earn. Further, a teenager can drop a level or more for choosing noncompliance. This is a logical consequence for failure to follow the terms of the previous level.

Permanent Level System

What about using a level system with a more permanent structure? You certainly can. The permanent level system is dependent upon the age and maturity level of the teenager.

Here is how it works. You first specify your child's rules and responsibilities. You also specify the privileges your child currently enjoys. For every instance of breaking a specified rule, or for failure to follow through on a responsibility, he loses one privilege. If he follows all of the rules and meets all of the responsibilities, he gets to keep and use all of his privileges. He may earn extra or special privileges with the use of a point system (discussed in a later section of this chapter).

When should the permanent level system be changed? When the rules and expectations change, or when the maturity level of the teenager requires a different set of privileges. I suggest you review the program with your child at least twice a year, and make adjustments accordingly. Here is an example for thirteen-year-old Tamara.

Rules and expectations for Tamara:

1. Pass all of your current class assignments with a letter grade of C or higher.

2. Be home for the night by 6 o'clock every weeknight.

3. Complete one major assigned chore once a week and all daily chores.

4. Never use obscene language or yell at anyone in the family.

Routine privileges for Tamara:

1. Can make (or receive) up to three ten-minute phone calls an evening.

2. Can stay up until 10 o'clock on school nights and until 11 o'clock on Friday and Saturday nights.

3. Can visit friends (or have them over) until 6 o'clock on school nights and until 10:30 on Friday and Saturday nights.

4. Can be allowed to go to the movies, the mall, religious services, school functions, parties, or other approved activities during the day and under adult supervision at night.

So how did Tamara do on the first week of the permanent level system? Her parents tracked her progress using the Rules Tracking Guide. She followed through successfully on rules 1, 2, and 3, but on Thursday she got into a screaming match with her brother over the use of the computer and called him several unprintable names. She lost all of her computer privileges for the day. On Friday she did not complete her major chore, which was to gather and load all of the towels, bed sheets, and white linen into the washing machine and then the dryer. She lost the chance to spend the evening at her friend's house and came in for the night at 6 o'clock. She spent the evening completing her laundry chore. However, Tamara did earn all of her other specified privileges for the week. The next week she avoided the problems of the first week and earned all of her privileges.

Tamara's seventeen-year-old sister has a permanent level system of her own. Her list of rules and expectations is different because she has different behaviors she is working on. Likewise, her list of routine privileges is different from Tamara's based upon her age and level of maturity. The older sister has a later bedtime, can engage in some activities at night without supervision, and has more freedom with friends and choices. As Tamara gets older and demonstrates more ability to make appropriate choices for herself, she too should be on a permanent level system with more freedom.

In this system of checks and balances, your teenager still has all of his or her *needs* met unconditionally: food, clothing, shelter, personal items, education, and expressions of love. At least some of his or her *wants* are met also. In order to secure special privileges beyond the routine ones, or things that are especially wanted, you can couple the use of the permanent level system with the point economy—which will be explained shortly. In order to increase its effectiveness, be sure to offer frequent praise and encouragement on how well the kid is doing on her system.

Finally, you can use the *shorthand version* of the level system, if you prefer. This version may prove especially useful for the generally compliant teenager. Your teenager is put on restriction for a week or a day for some misbehavior or rule infraction. However, she still must prove that she is trustworthy and responsible.

Linda

Linda, who is a generally trustworthy kid, has been in the house for three days now because she was sent up to the store to buy milk and loaf of bread, but instead she was talked into giving the money to her new friend so they could buy cigarettes. Linda came wandering in two hours past dinnertime, reeking of tobacco.

Linda realizes that she did something really stupid and has been apologetic. She has finished her time on grounding, but now will be given only a *small* amount of freedom out of the house. Today she gets to go out at 4:00 pm, and she has to be back home by 4:30 pm. If Linda handles that well she gets another half hour the next day, and the next. Linda then earns an hour, an hour and a half, and so forth, with no evidence of wrongdoing. Finally, by the end of the week Linda is back to the level of freedom out of the house she once enjoyed. What if Linda blows it? Then she goes back to the last level of freedom where she was successful.

The same idea holds true if you are restoring privileges after a short grounding. Your teenager gets his TV privileges back today, his phone privileges back tomorrow, and his friend visits the next day depending upon how he did today. The key is that at each step in the process, your child must now demonstrate he is trustworthy and responsible by making good choices.

Point Economies

The idea behind a point economy is simple: your teenager earns points based upon his behavior and the points are exchanged for privileges. The more points he earns, the more privileges he earns.

For example, you want your son to make his bed upon rising and have his bedroom in order before he leaves for school. You have a consequence rule about making the bed and keeping the room clean: if he doesn't do it on his own, you stand in the doorway while he does the chore. Now you add an incentive if he does the chore by awarding a set number of points for chore completion. Your teenager complies with the rule, avoids a consequence, and earns an incentive. The result is that you are much more likely to see the behavior change you want in a short time.

Point economies work best when you construct them with your teenager. The teenager's input regarding the incentive he would like to earn helps ensure success. Encourage your teenager to keep a parallel point chart so they can be aware of how they are doing during the day and week. Give extra points for keeping an accurate log.

You can establish point economies for:

- Routine and expected behaviors, such as chores, school attendance, and homework completion.

- Problem behaviors you want to see eliminated, such as arguing with parents, backtalk, smoking, or drug use.

- Behaviors you want to see more of, such as asking for help with homework, actively seeking to help others, speaking to others respectfully, learning about and performing independent living skills (money management, job search, shopping, cleaning, cooking, and so on).

You can occasionally give spontaneous points for behavior you liked as well. For example, your sons played video games for two hours without any name calling—ten points; your daughter didn't interrupt and argue while you were on your business call—ten points; your older daughter came right home and started on her afternoon chores—ten points.

Teenagers like the point economy because they can see a clear benefit to themselves. They are complying with family rules, avoiding unpleasant consequences, and earning something that they want. Parents like point economy because it increases child compliance, rewards wanted behavior that is likely to be repeated, and avoids conflict.

Jake's Point Chart

Behavior	Description	Deadline	Points	Earned
Up on time	Out of bed and bed made; showered, dressed; teeth brushed; hair combed	6:45 am	10	
School on time	Catch the bus; arrive at all classes on time	7 am–2:20 pm	10	
Daily Class Assignment Report	Complete the DCAR; have each teacher sign it; bring it home to parents	3 pm	10	
Homework	Complete all daily assignments when due	7 pm–8 pm	10	
Daily chores	Complete all assigned chores	6 pm, M–F	10	

To use a point economy effectively, link the giving of points with praise and acknowledgment. Be strict about the giving of points: either your teenager has performed the behavior and has earned the points, or she has not. Don't give half or quarter points, and don't give points for behavior that has not yet occurred. For each behavior, it is best to use a number such as ten. It is confusing and burdensome to give two points for this and seven points for that. Do not subtract points for noncompliance. Once the points are earned, they are earned; no behavior, no points.

Points need to be exchanged for privileges or incentives within a short time—that day or within a week. Just as the department store offers a two-for-one sale for a week's time, so should the incentive be relatively small and used close in time to when the desired behavior occurs.

Make a chart like the ones below of the behavior change you desire, a description of what you want to see, when it is supposed to happen, how many points it is worth, and if it was earned. Here are two examples.

This chart is for Monday through Friday. There are fifty possible points each day.

Jake's Incentives

If Jake earns the total fifty points for the day, he may have:

1. One additional hour on the computer

2. Fifteen additional minutes on his cell phone

If Jake earns at least 220 of the 250 points possible for the week, he may have:

1. The chance to be out with his friends on Friday night or Saturday in an approved activity

2. A movie pass

3. Ten dollars

For Rene, there are thirty points possible each day, plus another ten on Monday and Thursday.

Rene's Incentives

If Rene earns thirty points most days and forty points on Monday and Thursday, she may have:

1. Social network access on her computer for that day

2. A friend over or visit a friend until dinner time

Ways Teenagers Can Earn Extra Points

- Say please and thank you in a pleasant tone and show appreciation in other ways.
- Offer to help when you see that others need it.
- Ask for help instead of becoming frustrated and angry.
- Say something positive to someone or give a compliment.
- Follow through with requests the first time you are asked.
- Take responsibility for behavior choices by acknowledging mistakes.
- Do chores and homework without being reminded.
- Communicate with parents using problem-solving skills.
- Do not argue.
- Obey all rules.
- Do acts of kindness.

Rene's Point Chart

Behavior	Description	Deadline	Points	Earned
Stealing	Having a receipt for every item in her possession that is questioned	Parent review seven days / week	10	
Lying	Telling the truth when asked	Parent review seven days / week	10	
Check-in	Coming home on schedule; returning parent phone call on her cell phone within five minutes	Parent review seven days / week	10	
Chores	Preparing and cooking dinner	Mon. and Thurs.	10	

If Rene earns at least 200 of the 230 points possible for the week, Rene may have:

1. The chance to be out with her friends on Friday night or Saturday in an approved activity

2. Twenty dollars in art supplies

3. A weekly video rental

Contracts

A contract is a formal agreement between two or more people as to what each will do to fulfill the terms of the contract. A contract says if something takes place, something else will happen as a result that both parties have agreed to, or understand will happen.

Contracts are different from the rules and consequences that you use in a discipline plan. With a contract you and your adolescent come to an agreement each makes *voluntarily*.

Contracts do not work well with all kids. Adolescents who are vain and impulsive often do not do well with contracts, but some do. Further, kids who are addicted to chemicals, or deeply involved in crime, will often not do well with contracts, but some do quite well if the contracts are applied consistently. If you think you might need help, most therapists are familiar with contracting, and you may wish to enlist the help of one in devising a contract. The best advice is to try out a *small* short-term contract and monitor how well it works for you. If you have good success, try a larger, long-term contract.

Further, just like with rules, have a *small* number of contracts. You don't want to contract for every behavior that your child is capable of doing.

There are at least three different kinds of contracts you can use to formalize agreements between you and your teenager. These are: "if/then" contracts (sometimes called "contingency contracts"), "in-exchange-for" contracts (sometimes called "quid pro quo contracts"), and "good faith" contracts. All three contracts involve contingencies and consequences, but they work in different ways.

If/Then Contracts

If/then contracts can be written or oral. They have two parts, the specified behavior, the contingency ("if . . ."), and the consequence ("then . . ."), which is dependent on the contingency. I might make oral if/then contracts like these with my kids:

- Kayla, if you'll sweep out the garage, and neatly stack all of the boxes (the contingency), I'll pay you five dollars (the consequence).

- Andrea, when you've finished the dishes (the contingency), then you can go to the movies with Susan (the consequence).

- Jeff, if you come straight home from school every day this week and check in (the contingency), then I'll lift the rest of your grounding (the consequence), and you can go to the dance.

The contract must be worded so that both parties can see a clear connection between the specified behavior and the consequence: if *this* happens, *that* will happen; when *that* occurs, *this* will occur. But the contract is only as good as the will of both parties to follow it.

A written contract is best for more long-term events, or events that could happen more than once. It also has the advantage of being written and signed, with a copy to each party, which helps prevent arguments later over exactly *what* the contract specified. It can be worded just as an oral contract is.

You may have a written if/then contract for alcohol use, chores, homework, driving, or any number of other behaviors. You can write the contract during a meeting with the entire family.

In-Exchange-For Contracts

In-exchange-for contracts are those in which the *behavior* of one person is *dependent* on that of another. For example, you may agree to do your teenager's dinner dishes chore for one night in exchange for the teenager doing your garbage chore the next night. Or you may agree to drive your kids to the mall and give them a little spending money, if they agree to make dinner that night. You can also have a written in-exchange-for contract. You might agree to pay the tuition for your kid to attend equestrian camp this summer, if she agrees to provide babysitting for her little sister for three months.

With the in-exchange-for contract you are agreeing to make an exchange of behaviors that are predicated on the willingness of each person to strike a bargain. "You get what you want, I get what I want." But neither party gets what they want if one party doesn't live up to the agreement. Here are some examples:

- In exchange for weekly cleaning her room to an agreed upon standard, Mary will earn the privilege to hang one wall poster in her room (at her expense).

- In exchange for meeting for two hours a week with his math tutor, Joel will earn a movie pass. When he completes and turns in all of his math assignments for the week, Joel will earn a second movie pass he can use to take a friend to the movies.

- For every day that Cassandra does not talk back to her parents, she can place two fifteen-minute phone calls to her friends.

Good Faith Contract

Finally, there is the good faith contract, in which the behavior of one person is *independent* of that of another. You are simply saying this is what I what I intend to do, and are *consulting* with others (parents) and listening to any objections.

- Your adolescent may do as she pleases when she has completed all of her homework and chores.

- Your son will have a party at the house and will pay all of the expenses.

- Your daughter will go on the ski trip and will wrap her sprained ankle.

You can make a good faith contract with *yourself* that is not contingent on anyone else's behavior. You can have a written contract with yourself that you'll practice one of the new skills you're learning for one month. As an incentive, you will go see a movie at the theatre. Or you can make a good faith contract to get out of bed on Saturday or Sunday morning, get ready for religious services, and ask the kids to come along. As an incentive, you'll take yourself—and anyone who comes along—out for breakfast. Or you can make a contract with yourself to practice anger management skills for a month when the kids upset you. If you're successful you'll treat yourself to a round of golf.

Extending the idea of the good faith contract, you can write a contract involving you and your spouse. This contract is an agreement that pledges support for the other person. You simply say that you agree to the best of your ability to help the other parent in some specific ways. For example, you can write: "I will seek to not contradict you when you are giving a directive to the kids; I will compliment you on your using new parenting skills; comment approvingly on the progress I see the family is making; console you during setbacks; keep my doubts to myself; and strive to maintain a positive attitude." The incentive here is having a happier and healthier relationship with your parenting partner, as well as a greater likelihood of parenting success.

Contracts are very useful tools you can use to increase your odds of achieving behavior change with your teenager. Contracts are also tools that you may find useful in building bridges between you and your teenager, as well as you and your best intentions.

Contract Examples

The Jones family has three children: sixteen-year-old Sara, fifteen-year-old Jeff, and fourteen-year-old Kimberly. The Jones parents wish to write a contract for each of the kids to address certain behaviors. Here are the Jones family contracts:

For the Jones Family

If/Then Contract

Date: December 5, 20___

Date for review: February 2, 20___

Contracted behavior: Safe, responsible driving of personal car

Description of requirements: Sara Jones agrees to the terms of this contract between her and her parents.

1. Follow all the driving laws in our city and state.
2. Use my seatbelt at all times.
3. Obey the speed limit; not drive over the speed limit.
4. Not permit friends to drive my car.
5. Never drink alcohol and/or use drugs and attempt to drive the car, nor get into a car with anyone who has been drinking or using drugs.
6. Maintain the interior of the car, and have the car serviced on an agreed-upon schedule.
7. Maintain a B grade point average in school in order to retain my driving privileges.
8. Pay for all my own gas, oil, car wash, and repair expenses.
9. If I incur a traffic ticket, pay it in full before I am allowed to resume driving my car.

Contingencies:

1. If Sara violates any of the conditions set forth above, then she will forfeit all driving privileges for two weeks.
2. If her car is involved with any criminal activity (such as drinking and driving), then it will be put up for sale.
3. If Sara agrees to the requirements, then her parents agree to make her down payment, Sara's monthly car payment, and the car insurance payment for the next twelve months.
4. They also agree to let Sara drive the family to their vacation out of state next summer.

Teenager's signature: ___Sara Jones___

Parent's signature: ___Catherine Jones___

Parent's signature: ___Bill Jones___

In-Exchange-For Contract

Date: January 1, 20___
Date for review: March 15, 20___
Contracted behavior: Anger management
Description:

1. Jeff Jones agrees to attend weekly therapy sessions with his therapist, Dr. Phillip Smith.
2. Jeff agrees to be forthcoming with Dr. Smith, and to complete any homework assignments for anger management.
3. Jeff agrees to participate in a monthly family therapy session with the therapist.
4. Dr. Smith will be the judge of whether Jeff is fully participating in therapy.

Contingencies:

1. In exchange for Jeff attending all weekly sessions and participating fully in therapy as judged by Dr. Smith, during the next six weeks, he will earn the chance to try out for the high school wrestling team. His parents agree to purchase Jeff's wrestling equipment, attend all of his meets, and enthusiastically support the progress he is making in therapy and on the wrestling team.

Teenager's signature: ___Jeff Jones___
Parent's signature: ___Catherine Jones___
Parent's signature: ___Bill Jones___

Good Faith Contract

Date: May 10, 20___
Date for review: September 1, 20___
Contracted behavior: Notification of parties
Description:

1. I, Kimberly Jones, agree to give my parents forty-eight hours' notice if I wish to attend a party.
2. I will provide my parents with the names, address, and phone number of the people who are hosting the party.

3. I agree that my parents can make contact with the hosts to go over the details before giving consent for me to attend the party.

Teenager's signature: ___Kimberly Jones___
Parent's signature: ___Catherine Jones___
Parent's signature: _____Bill Jones_____

Using Incentives and Contracts Together

To use larger rewards over a longer period of time, keep a log of *all* the points your teenager has earned each week over the last four months. If the average is 90–100 percent of possible points your teenager has earned, then award a "bonus" reward; if an average of 80–89 percent of possible points, a slightly less desirable reward. The same idea if 70–79 percent of points are earned. Do not give anything for compliance under 70 percent. Use an if/then contract to specify the reward and percentage of points to be earned.

For example, Isaiah has a rate of 90 percent compliance over the last four months. He has contracted to go on a camping trip with his uncle for four days. If Isaiah had a rate of 80 percent, then the camping trip would be cut back to three days; with 70 percent compliance, it would be two days.

A sleepover for your teenager at the house would be for *this* many hours, guests, and activities, depending on the percentage of points earned. More points will get the teenager more hours, guests, and activities; fewer points results in fewer hours, guests, and activities.

The bonus incentives you award should be for more expensive or elaborate rewards for consistent compliance (but nothing extravagant). Examples might include a desired item, event tickets, or special trips, activities, or privileges. Offer these incentives once every four months, three times a year.

CHAPTER SIX

COMMUNICATION THAT GETS
THE RESULTS YOU WANT

Good communication requires, more than anything else, having good communication *skills*. This chapter will help you acquire those skills. Take your time to master each of the eight communication skills. Wait until you have mastered one through practice before adding another. To try to learn and use all the skills at once will be burdensome and confusing, and make you sound like a robot. The skills are:

- The five Bs of communication
- Social conversation
- Giving feedback
- Straight talk
- Taking notice
- Paraphrasing
- The "I" statement
- Asking for what you want

The Five Bs of Communication

The first set of skills is basic and essential to all communication with your adolescent. I call it the "five Bs of communication": Be specific, be clear, be behavioral, be brief, and be open. We'll look at what is involved in each one.

Be Specific

Stick to one issue at a time. You want to talk to your teenager about how he felt when his absent parent didn't call on his birthday. Avoid mixing in your personal feelings about the absent parent (what a louse he is, and how this is an example of how undependable he was when you were married, etc.). With unrelated issues, your message becomes confused and is lost. Better to focus on just the one issue, that is, your teenager's feelings about his parent not calling.

> *Not specific:* "Tim, too bad your dad didn't call. Want cake?"
>
> *Specific:* "Tim, I'd like to talk to you about your dad not calling on your birthday."

Be Clear

Learn to choose and weigh your words carefully. Cliché though it is, "Think before you speak" is nonetheless good advice. Choose words that convey acceptance and understanding. Avoid words that are heavily laden with emotions and tend to provoke anger or upset. Say what you mean in simple, plain language. You need not be profound, hysterical, or theatrical to get your message across.

> *Unclear:* "You'll have to pay all of your expenses."
>
> *Clear:* "You'll need to pay all of the gas, upkeep, and car insurance."

Be Behavioral

Talk about behavior, not attitudes. Behavior, or its effects, can be seen; attitudes cannot. It doesn't do any good to tell your teenager, "Improve your attitude toward your school work." What is it that you want your teenager to *do* or *not do*? If you want a change in behavior or wish to comment on behavior, you need to say what action you want or what effects you have seen.

Not Behavioral: "I want to thank you for all of your hard work today."

Behavioral: "I want to thank you for cutting the grass and raking the leaves. It was hard work and you did a super job."

Be Brief

Get to the point quickly. Most adolescents will tune you out when you sermonize, harangue, or shout. It is useless to say the same thing over again, only louder. Speak calmly and concisely. If you are too emotional, your teenager typically will not hear your words, only the anger, disappointment, sorrow, or other emotion. He will react emotionally to the emotion you convey, which does nothing to facilitate communication.

Not Brief: "I'm disappointed and sad that you broke up with Janet. But I understand that it was not your choice. I just wish young people today would learn to stick it out with a relationship when things get tough. Now, when I was your age . . ."

Brief: "I'm disappointed and sad that you broke up with Janet."

Be Open

Convey the opportunity for your teenager to speak *and your willingness to listen.*

Your teenager wants more than anything else to have someone listen and acknowledge her feelings. Acknowledgement is not the same as agreement. You may not agree with or be able to accept your teenager's message. Often that is not what your teenager is seeking; she does want someone to *listen.* With an open heart, ask her to tell you what she is thinking and feeling, and then listen with an open mind.

Not Open: "I can't believe you'd say that. Now, you don't really believe that, and you don't have any reason to think that way."

Open: "What I hear you saying is that you believe I am unfair and unreasonable."

With practice, you can master these five basic communication skills. Some parents make a deliberate attempt to practice the skills on a daily basis until they feel they are using them consistently. Other parents ask the teenager to help them practice the skills: during a five-minute conversation, the teenager is asked to take particular note of the things her parent says, and to note if they were specific, clear, behavioral, brief, and open.

As parents practice these communication skills (and others in this chapter), they often report that their kids start to imitate them. This is all to the good. Kids will imitate each other as well. The communication skills you teach your teenager by example will serve him well in his relationships with other people and over the course of their entire life. People cherish other people who are skilled communicators. As parents, being admired and respected for our excellent communication skills will help us in every other aspect of parenting.

Social Conversation

Having simple social conversation with your adolescent on a regular basis will pay handsomely not only in improving your communication skills as a parent, but also in strengthening the parent-teenager relationship. Good communication is the heart and soul of rapport.

Good conversation is more than just taking turns talking. Unfortunately, research shows that in the average American home, most "talk time" between adolescents and their parents is concerned with making requests and demands. Kids ask their parents for things or services, and parents make demands for things or services. Often the total talk time per week is reduced to a few minutes in the morning and again in the evening. When all parents hear are phrases like "Mom, I need a clean shirt!" and all the teenager hears is "If you need a clean shirt, you'll need to wash it yourself. I don't have time," there is little basis for building a relationship.

Listen more than you talk. A Greek philosopher once said: "We have two ears but only one mouth that we may hear more and speak less"—still good advice.

You can shoot the breeze while preparing dinner or during mealtime, while you're riding together in the car or while forsaking fifteen minutes of the evening news show. It doesn't really matter what the topic is—their day; your day; an incident that involved someone else; school; work; local, national, or world events; or even the weather—basically anything that you would talk with an adult about in the same fashion is appropriate.

Teenagers, like almost everyone, prefer to talk about themselves or things that interest them, which may not interest you. If you can get past this obstacle, let your teenager know you admire and respect him, or acknowledge some thought, talent, skill, or action he has taken. Talk in a friendly and positive manner. Finally, impose a one-minute gag rule on yourself. After speaking for one minute, stop and offer your teenager a chance to talk.

Open and Closed Questions

A useful tool to engage teenagers in conversation is to ask open questions. An open question is one that cannot be answered with a simple yes or no:

- What did you do in school today?

- What big plans do you have for the weekend?

- Who was that cute guy you were talking with at the basketball game?

You may still get a shrug or a one-word response, but by asking open questions you are much more likely to get a detailed response that could lead to a pleasant and interesting conversation with your teenager. People tend to like and appreciate people whom they know. Asking open questions in a friendly tone will help you get to know and have a likeable relationship with your teenager.

A closed question is just the opposite of an open question. You can answer it with one word: "How was school today?" Fine. "Learning anything interesting?" No. "Got any homework?" Yes. "Do you want chicken or hamburger for dinner?" Chicken. "Do you have soccer practice on Saturday?" Yes. "Anything new with your friends?" No. "Okay, anything you want to talk about?" No. (See? I try to talk to the kid and he never says anything!)

Of course, there is nothing wrong with closed questions—sometimes you need to ask them. To stimulate conversation, however, you need to vary closed questions with open ones.

Listening Cues

When you do engage your teenager in conversation, you want to let her know you are listening by using effective listening cues. Here is what you do:

- Maintain eye contact.

- Nod and smile occasionally.

- Lean forward slightly.

- Use an occasional encourager: "Uh huh. Interesting. Really? Is that so?"

Using these listening cues tells your teenager you are engaged in what she is saying, and you want to hear more. These cues open the door to quality communication.

Giving Feedback

At some point in your conversation with your teenager, you may want to offer feedback. Feedback simply means your turn to talk about what you think. Effective feedback is not critical; it is honest and straightforward. You get to offer feedback for being such a good listener.

There is no hard-and-fast rule about what you should say in giving feedback. You may want to offer advice, if it's asked for, or your own opinions or observations. You may offer possible solutions to problems or sympathy, if they're warranted. You may offer nothing more than acknowledgment, and paraphrase and summarize what you have heard. Sometimes the most effective feedback is to not make any comment at all, but only to listen, especially if the teenager is angry.

Further, not all feedback is verbal. A caring touch, hug, or kiss can say more than the most eloquent words. Likewise, sometimes a teenager's behavior says a great deal more than her words, and you can comment on that.

To describe the behavior you see, use feedback words like: withdrawn, fearful, anxious, upset, confused, hurt, worried, or angry; happy, excited, energetic, silly, pleased, or proud.

- You seem to be upset. Do you want to talk?

- Can I help you? You seem to be confused.

- You sure are happy today.

- You seem really excited.

- You look like you're lost in thought.

Most kids appreciate your noticing and being sensitive to their moods. Your feedback can also help them be aware of what they are thinking and feeling, which can lead to interesting conversations with you.

On the other hand, when teenagers will not talk to their parents, it's often not that they *can't* talk to them, it's that they are *fearful* of talking to them. Some kids are fearful of stinging criticism, the lash of the parent's anger, or the perception that when they do talk, they are misunderstood. Some kids simply do not have ready access to their feelings, or the words to articulate how they feel or want to say.

Most parents want to believe that they have made the opportunity to talk to them easy for their teenagers. To do this, you want to leave the door of opportunity wide open for them to come to you with their problems and concerns, failures and triumphs, hopes and plans, and to express their everyday needs, too. You want your teenager to have the certain knowledge that you will always have a receptive ear and a compassionate heart. When our children receive consistently positive and useful feedback from parents they will believe that they are being heard.

Here are some especially useful things to know about offering feedback to your adolescent:

- Be clear about the purpose of the feedback: "I wanted to comment on your plans for the party."

- Describe the specific behavior for which you are providing feedback: "I noticed that you didn't invite your brother to the party."

- Describe the consequences of her behavior: "I think he'll be hurt that you didn't invite him to the party."

- Ask for your teenager's response: "What do you think?"

- If a behavior change is sought, discuss the alternatives: "You could make a point of asking him yourself."

- Summarize, and then express your confidence and support: "So you'll talk to your brother as soon as he comes home from work and invite him to the party. I think that is a great idea and he'll be pleased."

Straight Talk

Someone once said, "The art of raising teenagers is stepping on their toes without messing up the shine on their shoes." In the same vein, the art of offering advice or criticism to teenagers is to convey it in a way that lets the teenager keep the shine on his shoes while he feels the pressure on his feet. Using the skill of straight talk will do this nicely.

Straight talk means that you say exactly what you think in behavioral terms. You say it straight, without hesitation or reserve; you use the five Bs of communication; and you leave out accusing or demeaning language. Here is an example of a parent and teenager using straight talk.

"Randy, I want to talk to you about your friends, and I want to use straight talk."

"Go ahead."

"My straight talk is that you've been very rude to several of your friends"

"When was this?"

"When you've had your friends over to watch the game the last several times. I've heard you call them some really nasty names."

"They know I'm just kidding."

"They may be hurt by it and may not want to say anything."

"They call me names, too. It's just fooling around."

"They may not want to say anything for fear of hurting your friendship. I think it is very rude and disrespectful and I would like you to stop doing it."

"Straight talk?"

"Go ahead."

"I think you are making too much of it. I don't mean it in a mean way. If my friends were hurt by it, they would tell me to knock it off. We know that we can say stuff like that to each other because we are friends."

"I would like you to stop doing it when you are around me."

"I can do that, Dad."

Now, how do you get your kids in the habit of hearing your straight talk? First, as the parent did in the example, you can *preface* your message by saying "straight talk?" This signals that what you are about to say is going to be frank and forthright. Second, you get the other person's *consent* to use straight talk. This way the person on the receiving end of the straight talk cannot deny that you have permission to speak freely and openly. Third, in order to *use* straight talk you must be willing to *hear* straight talk. Straight talk implies that you are willing to give as well as to receive information and engage in dialogue.

After using straight talk a few times, your teenager may say, "No, I'd rather not hear straight talk just now." That's okay. Remember, straight talk is designed to give advice or constructive criticism, not directives. It is a very handy communication tool that is respectful while at the same time being honest and straightforward. Like stepping on toes while maintaining shines.

Taking Notice

The only time some kids get feedback from their parents is when they do something wrong. In fact, the only way these kids know that their behavior has been pleasing to their parents is when they haven't been yelled at lately. This is not as it should be.

Take notice of the specific behavior that you like and want to see re-peated. Praise your teenager for this behavior as close in time as possible to when you first took notice of its occurrence.

Close in Time

"Hey, when I came in I saw you got the car washed. That's great."

"You're home right on time. Excellent."

"I see you cooked a wonderful meal for us. Thank you."

Use Feeling Words

Use feeling words such as "like," "appreciate," "glad," and "happy." Leave out "stinger" words or phrases: "I am so glad that you are doing that—*and it's about time you did*"; "I sure appreciate your *finally* being responsible."

Role Model

Teenagers take more frequent notice of what we *do* than what we *say*. Model the behavior you like and want to see your child repeat: speak cour-teously, help others, obey laws, complete chores and tasks, read books, listen attentively, attend religious services, and the like.

Spread the Word

Tell others what your teenager has done or is doing that you like. Lean over the fence and tell the neighbor what a great job he did trim-ming the shrubs. Talk about your teenager's success at family gatherings. Tell the teacher how proud you are of your daughter's homework and behavior in class. Word of your praise will get back to your kids. And, of course, praise them directly, such as at the dinner table when they can't help but hear. The easiest way to remember to offer praise is to take notice of the behavior you like and want to see repeated and comment on it.

Paraphrasing

Once you are engaged in active communication with your teenager, you'll want to use an occasional paraphrase. Paraphrasing is a powerful com-munication tool.

To paraphrase, use your *own* words to restate what you've heard your teenager say to you. As you gain experience using paraphrasing, you'll be able to reflect not only your teenager's words, but also the underlying feelings. This often helps your teenager clarify what he is thinking and feeling by having someone else listen and reflect what he said.

Helpful phrases to begin a paraphrase include:

"Sounds like . . ." "What I hear you saying is . . ." "Tell me if I understand . . ."

"Sounds like you are confused about what to do next."

"What I hear you saying is that you have three different course options and you are struggling a bit about which one to choose."

"Tell me if I understand. Dave and Jeremy have chosen to do this, and you want to be supportive of your friends, but you don't feel that this, all things considered, is the right choice for you."

Alternatively, you can comment on what you think the underlying feeling is that has been described:

"You were hurt and surprised when that happened."

"I'll bet that was exiting!"

"It must have been great to see Rick again."

If you have it wrong, don't worry, kids will tell you. Most kids appreciate your using an occasional paraphrase. It tells them you are actively listening and at least trying to understand what they are attempting to communicate to you.

The parents kids admire the most are the ones who they say "really listen" and "understand" their feelings and concerns. By using the skill of paraphrasing you'll earn just such a reputation with your teenager. This will pay huge dividends in your having a quality relationship with your teenager.

Echo Technique

Paraphrasing is a very useful tool but one that some parents find difficult to get the hang of with ease. While you are practicing, you might use a similar but easier tool called the echo technique. Simply repeat the last few words the teenager said. Here is an example.

"I don't feel like I can trust Vinnie anymore. He's lied to me too often. He says that he doesn't have any interest in Robin, they're just friends, but I've seen them walking together in the hallways and they look very cozy to me."
"Very cozy, okay."
"Yeah, and I know they like to text message each other all day."
"All day."
"Yes, so I'm thinking about talking to both of them. But I don't know if I'll do it separately or together. I just want to know where I stand."
"Where you stand."

You don't need to echo every phrase, but this communication technique is a good way to indicate to your teenager that you are actively listening and understanding.

The "I" Statement

Another useful communication tool is the "I" statement. An "I" statement has three interrelated parts:

- A behavior description

- Your feelings about the behavior

- Your want or need for behavior change

Here are two examples.

"Chris, when you are not dressed and ready to go in the morning, I feel very annoyed. I want you to be dressed and ready to eat breakfast by 6:30 am."

"Chris, I really appreciate your being dressed and ready to eat breakfast by 6:30 every morning this week. That's super. Now I need you to have all of your school supplies in your backpack and ready to go when we leave the house."

In an "I" statement you can say "I want . . . ," "I need . . . ," "I expect . . ." You're taking responsibility for your feelings when you do. You're telling the teenager (or spouse, relative, neighbor, friend, coworker) what you perceive is happening and you are *requesting* a specific behavior change.

Often, being made aware of how your behavior is affecting someone else is enough to motivate change, but not always. An "I" statement implies a choice, rather than being a directive. Telling your teenager you would like something to happen means there is still the option of doing it or not doing it. There is nothing wrong with stating a request or a desire, but an "I" statement will not mandate that your teenager (or anyone else) comply with your desires. If Chris doesn't give a rat's rear about his mother's annoyance with him wasting time in the morning, the "I" statement will fall on deaf ears.

The "I" statement usually works best with sensitive children who are sensitive to their parent's and other people's feelings and are considerate of other people's wishes. All they may need is to know what you want. "I" statements can be a very effective communication tool with kids like this.

Here is a simple script to use for the "I" statement: "When you . . . I feel . . . I would like/I need/I expect. . . . Thank you."

By using "I" statements, you can also model for teenagers how to ask for the things that they want. Kids (and parents) often *think* they are asking when they whine, complain, pout, threaten, cajole, cry, beg, guilt trip, or get angry. Through "I" statements they can learn how to state exactly how they feel about a situation directly to the person or people involved and ask them to make a change. They are often amazed at getting what they want—and so are parents.

Asking for What You Want

Communication quickly breaks down between parents and their kids when parents fail to ask for what they want. Unfortunately, some parents fail routinely, and by their example, teach their teenagers to do the same.

Sometimes when parents want a child to do something or to under-stand something, they use a shorthand version of mental telepathy that involves using their teenager's name coupled with an unclear demand: "Brad, knock it off!" "Oh, Ape-rull, stop that!" or, when they are especially exacerbated, they use all three names—"Juan Luis Ramirez, don't bug me!" Unless your child is quite adept at mind reading, this usually does little good. What exactly is it that you want the teenager to do or not do? How will he (and you) know that he is doing it?

There is a better way.

Minimal Effective Response

Start with an "I" statement. If your "I" message is ignored or disre-garded by your teenager, you may need to escalate your response. You can learn how to calmly and assertively ask for what you want by using a technique that psychologists David Rimm and John Masters called the "minimal effective response." The idea is that you use the minimal degree of effort to promote behavior change in someone else. To use this technique, say what you want in behavioral terms. If the message is disre-garded, you can calmly but assertively escalate the message until you get what you want. Here are a number of different ways a parent can respond to the same situation.

Unclear demand: "I'm studying, tone down the racket!"

Overkill: "I can't study! If you don't shut the hell up, you can't have your friends in the house for a month!"

Underkill: "Honey, please. I'm studying for an exam and I sure would appreciate it if you could keep the noise down just a teensy-weensy bit. Sorry to interrupt. Thank you. I love you."

The minimal effective response is a better alternative, escalating through the three statements to (c) as needed. Lead off with an "I" state-ment.

"When you and your friends make so much noise, I can't study for my exam. I want you and them to be quieter while I am studying. Thank you."

If this does not have the desired effect, use the minimal effective response.

a. "Look, I've asked you to please be more quiet. I simply cannot concentrate on my studying while the TV is so loud and your friends are talking."

b. "Turn down the TV and speak more softly while I am studying for my exam."

c. "Turn off the TV and go outside with your friends to talk."

When you ask for what you want in a firm and calm manner, you will usually get what you want—and avoid conflict—on the first try. However, by using the minimal effective response when the "I" message has failed to convey what you want, you can then escalate the message until the behavior change you want comes about. If you wind up getting into an argument, use the argument deflectors (page 111), or the script technique (below) to get your point across.

Script Technique

You can write a script for what you want to say and then repeat the script for different situations: a coming-home-after-curfew script, a cigarette/marijuana-smoking script, a do-your-chores/homework-now script, and so on. You can write out your script and read it aloud, or say it from memory when the time comes. Scripts are not sermonettes. Say what you want to say in the form of an "I" statement or a demand, simply, clearly, and quickly. Using this tool may seem a bit ludicrous at first, but it's better than becoming angry or overly emotional when you want to get your point across to your teenager and you can't find the words.

The five Bs of communication, plus open questions, listening cues, feedback, straight talk, social conversation, paraphrasing, the echo technique, "I" statements, the minimal effective response, and the script technique are all communication tools that stimulate, encourage, and promote parent-teenager communication. If you make the time and take the effort to practice using them, you will enjoy a quality relationship with your teenager.

Communication Blocks

Just as there are communication habits that encourage and stimulate communication with teenagers, there are two habits that block communication: parent deafness and coercion cycles.

Parent Deafness

Parents can literally train a child to ignore them. A teenager who is parent deaf is deaf to parental demands. It is not that he doesn't hear—he hears fine—it is that he has been trained not to respond. The teenager knows from experience that when Mom or Dad says that something needs to happen, it doesn't. Mom and Dad don't mean what they say and say what they mean. The demand can be safely ignored.

Most parentally deaf teenagers start losing their hearing when they are very young. The deafness then accelerates when they become adolescents. The three-year-old is told not to do some obnoxious behavior . . . and told, and warned, and threatened, and told again. Finally, the parent gives up and the child does as he pleases.

As the child gets older, she learns from experience she doesn't really have to come to the dinner table on the first call, she doesn't really have to be in by curfew, and she doesn't really have to do the chore if she doesn't feel like doing it. She also learns that she doesn't need to respond until her parent calls her to the dinner table for the fifth time, nothing will happen as a result of staying out three hours past curfew, and her parents will do the chore because it is easier that way. The child learns to extrapolate from these experiences and discovers it is "okay" to talk back to her parents, that she can skip school, smoke dope, and date any boy she wants, because her parents no longer bother to put a stop to it. Mom and Dad do not say what needs to be said, and do what needs to be done. The result is children that are deaf to their parents' demands.

How do you get your kids to hear you? The cure for parent deafness is consistency, clarity, and follow-through.

Consistency means consistently giving the same message every time. If your teenager must comply this time but not the next, the resulting inconsistency on your part breeds disbelief in, and contempt for, your parental word.

Clarity means being clear. Telling your teenager to "knock it off," "stop it, I said," and "quit doing that or you'll be sorry" tells them nothing. Specify the behavior that you want to see altered in the demand.

Follow-through means imposing consequences immediately. Nothing gets our attention like results. Nothing underlines our message like follow-through. When teenagers learn that they are consistently choosing a negative consequence that goes with the negative behavior, they then alter their behavior in their own best interest.

Coercion Cycles

Sometimes parents and kids find themselves circling around the same issues again and again. This is usually because parents and teenagers are in a cycle of failed communication. The parent never gets her point across to the adolescent, and the adolescent never strives to get the point. Instead, parent and teenager play a communication game where both wind up feeling angry and alienated from one another. Psychologist Gerald Patterson calls these wacky communication breakdowns *coercion cycles*. The common elements of coercion cycles include: anger and irritation, denial and defensiveness, and placating and appeasement.

Scott

Scott's mother walked into the house carrying a full bag of groceries from the car. She was hot and tired and had decided that supper would be a frozen dinner this evening. As she peered into the living room she could see Scott sprawled out on the couch, watching that damn MTV, with his dirty socks propped up on the armrest. That did it.

"Scott! What are you doing?"
"I'm watching TV."
"You're supposed to be watching your little brother, not TV."
"I am watching him."
"Is he in his room?"
"He's around."
"Where is he exactly? Josh is only four years old. I wish you would be more responsible."
"He's around."

"Go look for him."

"I will as soon as this is over."

"Is he in his room?"

"He's around."

"As long as he's in his room, that's fine."

"He is."

"Okay then. Do you want the roast beef or the turkey loaf?"

As Scott's mother began to place the frozen dinners in the microwave oven, Josh came running into the house from the backyard. She told Josh to wash his hands for dinner. Josh ran into the living room and began to ride his tricycle in circles. Scott was watching a video of a young woman with blue hair and wearing a spiked dog collar, who was screaming into a microphone about wanting freedom from oppression. It was only after dinner that Mother discovered that Josh had decided to repaint the outside walls with a red permanent marker.

Kelly

Kelly was excited. She was sure that she would be getting her running shoes—the ones with the little red lights in the soles. Kelly's father examined the shoes when Kelly handed them to him with a pleading look on her face. The shoes looked fine—until Dad saw the two hundred dollar price tag hanging from the shoelaces.

"What? Two hundred dollars! I don't think so, Kelly."

"Dad," Kelly explained patiently, "these are special, I need them."

"Need them for what? You're not a track star."

"I need them for school."

"Why does a seventh grader need two hundred dollar running shoes to wear to school?"

"Dad, you want me to look like a dork? Everyone is wearing these."

"Why is everybody wearing these?"

"Because they're cool, that's why," Kelly said with rising exasperation.

"Kelly, we can't afford these shoes."

"But I need them."

"What is the matter with these shoes over here?" Dad asked in a reasonable tone as he moved over to a counter with fifty dollar sneakers. "You can have one of these."

"Why?" Kelly asked. "Why do you always make me take the lousy stuff?"

"Kelly, I don't . . ."

"Yes, you do!" Kelly started to cry. "I never get anything!"

"Honey, two hundred dollars is half of our school clothes budget."

"Dad-dee! Pleazzzzzze! I need them."

"Oh, Kelly. Please don't make a scene. Let's have lunch, then come back and finish our shopping, okay?"

Kelly began to wail.

"Kelly. . . ."

Kelly began to stagger around the aisle under the weight of her grief. People were looking.

"Kelly. . . . Okay, Okay, Okay, if it means that much to you. Let's get the damn shoes."

Kelly's tears started to subside. She began to feel better. Now she could look cool—especially at night when everybody could see the little red lights in the soles of her ultra cool two hundred dollar shoes. As they walked up to the register, and as Dad took out his credit card, he realized that he felt exhausted and broke. But hey, at least Kelly was happy, and he wouldn't let this happen again when they got to the jeans department.

Coercion Cycles Stopped

The antidote to coercion cycles is the five Bs of communication. That is framing your communication to your adolescent in words that are specific, clear, behavioral, brief, and open. Let's replay these scenes.

Scott

"Scott! Are you watching your little brother?"

"Yeah, I'm watching him."

"Where is he right now?"

"He's in his room."

"Do you know that for certain?"

"Yeah, he's in there."

"I want you to get up off the couch, go look for him, and then come and tell me where he is and what he has been up to."

"I will as soon as this is over."

"No, Scott. Now. Please do it right now."

Mother stood in the doorway of the living room with an icy stare until Scott, with a heavy sigh and rolling eyes, got up off the couch and went to look for Josh

"Thank you for your cooperation," Mother said. "Do you want the roast beef or turkey loaf?"

"Turkey loaf," Scott said, as he came through the kitchen on his way to the backyard. A minute later Josh came running into the kitchen from outside. His mother told him to go into the bathroom to wash his hands. Josh raced toward the living room. His mother followed him. Scott walked in behind Josh.

"He was in the yard, with markers in his hand," he said.

"Josh, go to the bathroom and wash your hands with the bar soap. Get all of the dirt off your hands, rinse them, and then dry them with a towel. Then come in and sit at the kitchen table."

Josh ran toward his tricycle.

"Josh, do it now. If you need help, Scott will help you do it."

Josh climbed carefully off his tricycle and walked slowly to the bathroom. Josh and Scott looked at each other. What was going on? On the way, Josh and Scott heard their mother say, "As soon as dinner is over, Scott, you clear the table and stack the dishes in the dishwasher, and Josh, you go out to the backyard and bring me all of your permanent markers."

Both boys rolled their eyes. It was that stupid parenting class.

Kelly

Kelly's dad howled, "What! Two hundred dollars! I don't think so, Kelly."

"Dad," Kelly explained patiently, "these are special. I need them."

"Do you need them for school? We are only buying school clothes right now."

"Well. . . . Yeah. I need them for school. They're cool."

"Yes, I can see that they're cool, and that you really want them. And the reality is that we can't afford to spend this much on one item."

"Why not?"

"Because we can't afford to spend this much on one item."

"But Dad. . . ."

"You can spend fifty dollars on any pair of sneakers that you like."

"But what about these? I don't want to look like a dork."

"Then I suggest you find a pair that you like that are within our price range."

"But Dad. . . ."

"I'm going over to the jeans section while you find a pair of sneakers you like. I'll meet you over there."

"Well, can I at least get a pair of designer jeans?"

"Sure can, as long as you can find a pair that is within our price range."

"Holy cow. I'll shop with Mom from now on."

Being clear, calm, and assertive with teenagers will keep you and them out of coercion cycle entanglement.

CONFLICT RESOLUTION WITH TEENAGERS

Some conflict in families is inevitable; but *continual* conflict and angry encounters with your adolescent are not. Consistent use of the skills in this chapter will help you avoid conflict most of the time. Many problems with teenagers are mundane and only require a willingness to problem-solve and seek solutions that everyone can live with. Like all of the other skills in this book, with practice, you *can* do this.

The following skills go a long way to facilitate conflict resolution and problem-solving:

- Solving specific problems

- Intentional listening

- Balancing *yes* and *no*

- Workable solutions

Solving Specific Problems

A useful tool to use when attempting to problem-solve an issue is a Problem-Solving worksheet (provided on the website). The key is that you and your teenager will work together on this, with mutual respect and a willingness to find solutions. To create a Problem-Solving Worksheet, follow these steps:

1. Write a short description of the problem in behavioral terms.

2. Working with your teenager, write three or four ideas for possible solutions.

3. Each of you mark whether you think each possible solution will work, might work, won't work. Discuss your reasons, taking into account the possible consequences of each choice.

4. Continue to discuss, writing down more ideas if needed, until you both agree on a particular solution. If you simply cannot agree, then put off making a decision until another day.

5. Implement the solution you decide on and schedule a time within a week to a month to review how it's going. Make any needed changes.

6. When you and your teenager become proficient at using the worksheet, you can follow the same procedure orally—simply follow the first five steps—and dispense with using the worksheet, if you like.

This is how one family problem-solved an ongoing issue:

1. Describe the problem in simple, clear, direct, behavioral terms:

> There is a problem with the house lights being left on after everyone has left for the day. When the lights are left on, it runs up the electric bill beyond what we can afford and is an unnecessary expense.

2. Brainstorm and write down three or four possible solutions:

   a. Assign one person the job of turning off all the lights before leaving the house.

   b. Have each person turn off the lights he/she turned on upon leaving the room.

   c. Get automatic timers for all the lights.

   d. Budget more money for the light bill each month.

3. What will work, might work, won't work:

   a. That will work, but it isn't fair for the same person to have to do it all the time. We would need to rotate the responsibility. And each person needs to agree to be aware of the lights they turn on, and strive to turn them off.

   b. That could work, but isn't working now, so we have the problem.

   c. That's too expensive; we are already struggling to pay the light bill.

   d. The same problem with as with (c).

4. Agree on a solution you think will work.

   It looks like (a) is the answer. The last person to leave the house each day checks the rooms to be sure that the lights are out. We'll put a reminder note on the front door. Each person in the family will have the task for one week. We all agree to strive to be aware of the lights we turn on, and then turn them off when we leave the room.

5. Begin using the solution. Review and make any needed changes.

   Hooray! The electric bill is down 20 percent this month. However, we are still having lights left on in the back bedrooms. Let's post a reminder note by the door in every room and see if that makes a difference. Let's celebrate our success and go weekend camping.

This problem-solving approach is simple, but very effective. It provides everyone in the family an opportunity to be heard and to contribute directly to the family's success.

Intentional Listening

Listening during conflict resolution and active problem-solving requires that you listen with two ears, as well as a third. Listen for *why* your teenager thinks as he or she does about the issue. Listening in this way requires an open mind and constant effort. It is hard, but certainly worth your attention. Listen in these three ways:

Listen with an Uncritical Mind

Try not to make up your mind about what is on your teenager's mind before he says it. Let your teenager say what he wants to say, no matter how stupid, insignificant, or wrong you may think it is at the time.

Listen with Acceptance

Be aware of your body language so that you convey respect. A smirking mouth, bored grin, folded arms, heavy sighs, and glaring/rolling eyes will short-circuit your adolescent's desire to communicate. Instead, while maintaining eye contact and nodding occasionally, lean forward slightly, with your arms resting on your knees.

Listen with Interest

You can demonstrate interest when you paraphrase responses and ask open questions. Asking a question implies that you will wait for an answer. When you hear a statement or an opinion with which you disagree (even strongly disagree), ask your teenager to elaborate and to expand on his answer.

When you don't understand his point, use an encouraging phrase such as "I don't think I understand, but please keep going." Another helpful phrase is "Help me see the other side of this if you do not agree with what I've said about it." Using these phrases *alone* will greatly strengthen the chances that your teenager will *listen* to *you* and what you have to say about the issue.

Further, in your own mind, seek to separate fact from subjective opinion. "Charlie, you're a slob" is an opinion. "Charlie, you left your dirty clothes on the bathroom floor" is a fact. Kids will frequently argue and not listen to opinions about themselves; it is much harder to argue with a fact.

Listening in these three ways will earn you a reputation with your teenager as a parent who listens respectfully and accurately. This reputation alone can help solve problems.

Workable Solutions

There are a number of well-known and commonsense positions you can assume in negotiating or collaborating that could provide workable solutions to problems with your teenager. They are all based on mutual respect and a willingness to cooperate. Matthew McKay, Martha Davis, and Patrick Fanning developed part of the list in their book, *Messages: The Communication Skills Book.*

> Take turns: "I'll take out the garbage on the even-numbered weeks if you'll take out the garbage on the odd-numbered weeks."
>
> Split the difference: "You want me to buy you a new bedroom set. I'll pay half if you'll pay the other half."
>
> Have a trial period: "You can try doing your homework in your room for a month. If your grades drop in any subject, it's back to the kitchen table."
>
> Cut the pie: "I've made up a list of household chores. Everyone can take turns choosing from the list until all of the chores are picked."
>
> You get what you want, I get what I want: "You can have the party at the house as long as you pay the expenses, and there is responsible adult supervision."
>
> Do both: "You can spend Christmas Eve with me and Christmas Day with your mom."

Balancing Yes and No

Ideally, children should hear a balance of *yes* and *no* responses from their parents. Kids never say, "You always say yes! You always let me do everything I want to do. It's not fair." They tend to remember the *no* and forget about the *yes.*

It is not the firm *no* that upsets most teenagers; it is the superior or hostile tone in which the parent states it: "Huh, you've got to be kidding!"; "Hell no"; "Don't even think about asking me that"; "I said no, and that's the end of it"; "In your dreams, fella"; "What part of *no* don't you understand?"

It is better to let your *no* be a *no* and to not dress it up with commentary. Just give a simple *no* and a brief explanation, if one is warranted: "No, you can't be out that late on a school night"; "No, that is against the rule"; "No, that is not acceptable to me." Often, a simple *no* will do nicely. Sometimes kids ask just to be sure that the answer really is *no*.

Saying *yes* is easy (and usually a lot more fun). However, you can qualify your *yes* to make it more explicit as to what you are giving consent to. You can use this phrase: "Yes, but here is what needs to happen. . . ." ("Yes, but here is what needs to happen when you drive my car. Your friends cannot drive the car and you need to put at least ten dollars in the gas tank.") You can also use the word *and* instead of the word *but*: "Yes, you can go to the movies with Ramon, and you need to be home before 11 o'clock"; "Yes, I am fine with you finishing your game first and you need to empty the trash." Elaborating on the *yes* in this way will help prevent misunderstanding, conflicts, arguments, and hurt feelings later on.

REINFORCERS FOR BEHAVIORS YOU WANT TO SEE REPEATED

Why can't parents simply depend upon the avoidance of the adverse consequence to deter teenage behavior? Isn't that enough to get kids to behave better? For most kids it is not, especially if the misbehavior has a number of built-in incentives to choose it.

I once worked with a family in which the sixteen-year-old daughter was being grounded a week for every day of school that she skipped out on. The girl was frustrated, the school was frustrated, and the parents were frustrated because their daughter's behavior in this regard had not improved one bit. Everybody was mad at everybody else.

The key to the solution to this attendance problem was to ask the family a simple question: how long was Michelle grounded for right now? Michelle replied wearily, "Six months." Her mother said, "No, honey, I think it's only four months." Her father, wanting to be helpful, said, "Geez, I thought it was five months."

Just as I thought, no one in the family had the slightest idea. Each day when she got home from school, Michelle was told by one of her parents that the school had called and reported her truant from one or more of her classes. The resulting penalty was that Michelle racked up another week on grounding. This meant no TV, phone, text messaging, visits to or from friends, computer surfing, social outings, or recreational activities of any kind. And yet Michelle kept skipping.

Michelle the Truant had not the slightest incentive to attend school. In fact, she had very good reason, from her perspective, to cut out after first period or before: she could then play the rest of the day. She could do all of the things she could never possibly do while she was living in a black hole of restriction. She visited her friends, went shopping, saw movies, and played on the beach on sunny days.

As it was, Michelle had no reasonable prospect of digging herself out of an ever-deepening hole, so why try? (Her lack of education was of little concern as she was going to be a rock star.)

We wiped the slate clean and started again. I set the family up with a simple contract: for every day that Michelle attended all of her classes and did satisfactory work, she could have free time to do with as she pleased that evening and weekend. For every instance of truancy or unsatisfactory work, her parents would restrict her freedom for that evening or the weekend, and monitor makeup schoolwork. Michelle's parents tracked her attendance and schoolwork with the Daily Class Assignment Report (provided on the website). After Michelle skipped twice in the next three weeks—testing the system, as it were—and her parents followed up, she never cut school again. She graduated with her class and today she is a young mother with kids of her own to get to school. (She never became a rock star, however.)

Recognizing Positive Behavior

Every teenager does things that are cooperative, appropriate, and expected—at least some of the time. No one (not even a teenager) is a pain in the neck all of the time. We have, up until now, been emphasizing methods to get your teenager to discontinue negative behavior and to choose positive behavior as an alternative. Now I want to show you some very effective skills that will greatly increase the chances of your teenager choosing not only to *not* do the wrong thing, but also to *do* the right thing.

You and I would not work at our jobs unless we are paid a salary. We also want our medical benefits, vacation days, days off, coffee breaks, chance for promotion with more freedom, and retirement plans. In addition to money, these are our rewards and incentives for proper job performance. We earn these things in exchange for our labor. In the same way, teenagers can earn rewards and incentives from their parents for appropriate and expected behavior.

Which is better? "Katie, here is the concert ticket that you wanted. In exchange, I want you to promise not to smoke cigarettes this month," or "Katie, you can earn the money to go to the concert if you can get through the month without any evidence of smoking cigarettes"?

In the first instance, Katie has no incentive to stop smoking; in the second she has definite incentive. This does not mean that Katie's smoking behavior will not still be tracked and monitored—it will be—it simply means that Katie can earn a positive incentive *as well as* avoiding a negative consequence for not smoking. We are literally telling the child that they can avoid the negative *and* choose the positive; they can avoid a negative consequence *and* earn a positive consequence.

Incentives must have meaning to the teenager in order to be effective. The reward must be something that is tied directly to the desired behavior and is something that the teenager wants or is willing to expend the effort to obtain.

"Billy! A whole week of staying clean and sober; let's go out for ice cream!" will not do. "Billy! Your urinalysis test came back clean. Congratulations on your success. As we agreed, you can go to the football game tonight with your friends" is more like it.

It is not enough to only attempt to deter negative, unwanted behavior; we must work to encourage positive, wanted behavior as well. As parents we want to consistently strengthen the occurrence of behavior we like and want to see repeated, and weaken and put the brakes on behavior we want to see ended. The best way to do this is to make it easy for the teenager to choose what psychologist Alan Kazdin calls the "positive opposite" of what they were choosing before. Incentives make that happen.

Rewards need not be expensive or elaborate to be effective.

"Jimmy! You did a great job bundling up all the newspapers. Here is a Rolex watch. Enjoy!" is absurd. "Jimmy! You did a great job bundling up all of the newspapers. I appreciate that" will do.

Wait a minute, what about the reward? Jimmy has his reward—my thanks and recognition for a job well done. This kind of reward is perfectly fine. In fact, most kids want praise and recognition from their parents as much or more than any tangible reward.

Praise

Praise is the single most effective way to reward positive behavior and to reinforce the likelihood of its being repeated. If you want your teenager (or your spouse, coworker, relative, or friend) to repeat a positive behavior that you like, then praise him for it. This is true whether someone is two years old, or ninety-two years old.

Praise is best when it is *limited, specific,* and *given sincerely.* This is as it should be because it is reflective of how things are in the larger world. Our boss doesn't praise us to the skies every morning when we show up for work on time. However, she may comment on it and we may earn a written notice in our evaluation that we are punctual. That tends to make us want to be punctual.

Nor do you want to praise any and every behavior that your child is capable of doing ("Hey, great breathing today; keep it up!"). But you do want to take notice of and praise a positive behavior that the teenager is establishing: "I noticed that as soon as you came home from school you feed the dog. That's cool."

Think about the teacher at your teenager's school for whom the kids will walk on hot coals to please. Not only does that teacher tend to set high standards, but he or she also tends to consistently praise students for every achievement connected to those standards. The teacher's praise is limited to the issue of schoolwork, is specific to what she found praiseworthy, and is given sincerely because he or she wants to see the behavior repeated: "Jonathan, your science project was turned in right on time. Excellent. I really like the way you illustrated the chambers of the heart. I enjoy reading your reports and it is a pleasure to have you in class. Very fine work, indeed."

As in the example, in order for praise to be effective, you need to limit your praise to the circumstance at hand, and sincerely and specifically say what it is that you appreciate or admire that the teenager has done. Don't say, "Good job on the kitchen"; instead say what you like and appreciate: "I see that you have all of the dishes washed and put away, the counters cleaned, and the floor swept—very nicely done. I appreciate your having it all done before we need to leave for the game. It is a pleasure to be able to rely on you."

Avoid Mixing Praise with Criticism

When you praise, withhold criticism. "I see that you have all of the dishes washed and put away, the counters cleaned, and the floor swept—very nicely done. I just wish you hadn't waited until almost game time to start doing it. Let's see if you can do better next time, okay?" Right. In this instance, your teenager will very likely remember the criticism and ignore the praise. The probable result is that the next time you want the kitchen cleaned, she will think, "Why should I? All I get is criticized for it."

Mixing Constructive Criticism with Feedback

There is nothing wrong with criticism. Often it is how we learn to do better. However, the most useless criticism for anyone is stinging criticism given when no corrective action can be taken: "Why did you leave your bike outside unlocked? Don't you realize how easy it is for someone to steal it? That was a damn fool thing to do."

Feedback, on the other hand, is a process for giving useful information. You can help your teenager do better consistently by combing useful information with feedback: "You left your bike outside unlocked and someone stole it. That was an unfortunate choice on your part. If the police recover your bike, or you use your savings to buy another one, get a secure lock or bring the bike into the house after you ride it." In this case, you are criticizing the teenager's behavior choice—not the teenager—and you are giving useful information about how he can do better, which will give you an opportunity to praise him or her in the future.

Praise in public for all to hear; give constructive criticism in private for only one to hear. Never criticize your teenager in front of an audience. If you do the kid will likely play to the audience in order to save face. Instead, wait for a time when you are alone and away from the situation. Then calmly say what you like, and what you do not; what you want to see more of, and what you want to see less of. Praise with a good deal more frequency than you give criticism.

Praise the character traits or behavior patterns you want to see more frequently. The best way to do this is to describe the specific positive behavior you are aware of or see.

- You made some very intelligent and mature choices about not getting into a car with someone who has been drinking.

- I appreciate your willingness to jump right in and help us with the yard work. Your work helped us finish much faster.

- You are a very kind and thoughtful person to volunteer your time to read to the kids at the library.

Combine Praise with Physical Affection

Another thing you can do that will reinforce your praise is to combine it with expressions of physical affection. As you praise your teenager, give her a hug, or a kiss, or both. If you can't hug or kiss, you can put a hand on her shoulder, or even just make eye contact.

Combine Praise with Formal Rewards

Praise should be the primary way in which we seek to reinforce positive behavior, but it's not the only way. Giving your teenager formal rewards and incentives for positive behavior is a good way, too.

Many parents bristle at the idea of offering their misbehaving kids rewards and incentives for proper behavior—as well they should. It is useless and counterproductive to attempt to stop negative behavior with positive rewards. This tactic doesn't work and is psychologically destructive to both the parent and the teenager. Don't do it.

Instead, use positive rewards to reinforce positive behavior. There is a world of difference between the two. Formal rewards and incentives are very effective in increasing *positive* behavior. They are totally ineffective in decreasing *negative* behavior, and so should never be used for that purpose. Consider the difference between a movie *pass* and a movie *ticket*.

It's Saturday morning and Sam wants to study for a test that could lead to a job promotion. His thirteen-year-old son has been an obnoxious hellion all morning. Sam gives his son the money for a movie ticket so he can get him out of his hair for a few hours.

Good Parent Sam has consequently done nothing more than reinforce his son's obnoxious behavior, because it has lead to a free movie. The unwitting message to his son is that the next time he wants to attend a movie, all he has to do is act up. He has learned the power of coercion cloaked in the art of extortion.

Rosa's thirteen-year-old son has been trustworthy and responsible by getting all of his point charts for the week. She rewards him by giving him a weekly movie pass.

See the difference? The first example is a bribe. The second is an earned reward. A bribe is never earned. A reward must be.

A parent can also give spontaneous rewards in addition to earned ones. Say, "Because you've been so helpful around the house, let's stop for a banana split," not, "If you'll stop screaming in my ear while I'm driving, I'll buy you a damn banana split!"

Children learn what we teach them. When we reward them, even inadvertently, for negative behavior, they are very likely to repeat it. When we deliberately reward them for positive behavior, they will repeat that as well. That is the way behavior works.

We have all made the mistake of rewarding negative behavior with positive rewards. You've done it, our parents have done it, and I have certainly done it. One reason is because it is harder to think of ways to reward a teenager than it is a younger child.

If my four-year-old can get through the candy section of the grocery store without throwing her usual tantrum, she may get a piece of sugarless candy when we get to the car. If she eats all of her dinner, she can have a dessert. And if she brushes her teeth, gets her jammies on, and into bed without a fuss, I'll come in and read her a story. My fourteen-year-old isn't likely to be too thrilled when I come in to read her a bedtime story. However, if she too gets to bed on time, I will tape her favorite late night show so she can watch it the next day.

Ask your teenager what he or she would find appealing as a possible reward. For most adolescents, this will involve either time or money, such as extra spending money or the freedom to go and do something special.

Kinds of Rewards

There are at least four categories of rewards that can be used to help change teenagers' behavior: social, activity, material, and unconditional. Rewards can be given daily, weekly, or at the moment.

Social Rewards

Social rewards certainly include praise and recognition, but they also include spending quality and fun time together with other people, including parents. In addition to spending time with friends and other peers, have the teenager spend time with you. Going on a picnic, playing a game, and going out to dinner and a movie are all good ways to reward the teenager's positive behavior.

Activity Rewards

Activity rewards are designed to make the adolescent's free time contingent upon the positive use of her scheduled time. If she has used her school time appropriately and completed her household chores, then she should have free time in the evening, on weekends, and during vacation time for pleasurable activities: playing video games, watching TV, visiting friends, or doing as she pleases. The critical link is that extra free time be first *earned*, not first *given*.

- Every time you complete all of your homework, you can do as you please until bedtime.

- When you have finished all of your chores, you can go out with your friends.

- For every task you complete, you can earn an extra twenty minutes on your computer or cell phone.

Material Rewards

As the name implies, material rewards are given in the form of money or things that cost money. We can give our kids money or an allowance and require nothing more from them than that they continue to draw breath, or we can make the giving of money conditional upon their positive behavior. Certainly, teenagers can do extra chores around the house, work in your business, or secure a part-time job to earn money, but if we want to use money as a motivator, use it on a contractual basis: when *this* happens, *that* will happen.

- When you can pull your GPA up one letter grade, I'll go in halfway with you on a car we choose together.

- If you complete this list of extra chores, and after I've checked to make sure they are done satisfactorily, I'll pay you ten dollars for each one.

- If you watch your little sister tonight while your mom and I go out, we'll pay the minimum wage.

It is perfectly all right to reward money that goes directly into a kid's checking account or savings account. Many teenagers learn quickly how to manage their spending habits when they must rely on a bank account to make purchases. You can also give money for birthdays and holidays or for other special purposes. Just be sure that your teenager has ample opportunity to earn money as well.

Unconditional Rewards

Unconditional rewards are the most fun to give and to receive. You can give them for *general, positive* behavior that you want to see repeated. Since your child never knows when he or she will receive one, these rewards tend to be very reinforcing.

- Hey, you guys were so helpful at the family barbecue; I thought we'd have your friends over next weekend for another one.

- You made the honor roll and I am very proud of you. I'd like to have your certificate framed and put up in the living room.

- I have been so pleased with your willingness to share the computer time with your brother and sister. Let's get that upgrade that you wanted.

It is fine to use more than one type of reward, such as mixing praise with a material reward. It is also a good idea to keep a mental note of what kind of reward your teenager seems to respond to most consistently, and to use that.

Twelve Ways to Show Love and Affection

Praise

Praise is the single most powerful way to encourage and support positive behavior. If you want to see a teenager repeat a certain behavior, praise him for it. Praising means that you love enough to do it. If your teenager does not respond well to praise, use acknowledgment.

Acknowledgment

To acknowledge means to recognize what is in a positive way. Compliments are good ways to acknowledge your adolescent: "Wow, I like that haircut. That looks good." You can also acknowledge without putting a positive spin on it: "I see you got your math assignment done." Acknowledgment means I've taken notice because I care so much about you.

Expressions of Affection

Some parents say "I love you" easily and often; others find it difficult or awkward. But every teenager needs to hear his parents say it, preferably at least once a day. The same is true of hugs and kisses: some kids (and parents) who would be embarrassed with a sugary "I love you" can get the same message with a kiss or hug.

Touch

A light touch on the shoulder or the hand can have a calming and soothing effect, and also convey the message "I love you." Interestingly, research has found that people are almost universally much more likely to be cooperative and helpful to others when they are touched than when they are not. Touch is a powerful device for making emotional contact.

Listening with Empathy

Listen accurately and with compassion when teenagers are in distress. Listen to their words, and then give voice to the underlying feelings. Listen with deep-seated concern, with the same wounded heart. Listening in this manner is a wonderful way to express your love.

Spending Time Together

Spending time as a family and separately with each child in the family gives families a strength and solidarity that is vital. Spend time with your teenager going on short trips, attending religious services, seeing places of interest, attending sporting or cultural events, or going out for planned and unplanned activities. Even if you must schedule the time or sacrifice your own time, it is important that you follow this practice as a means of expressing your love to your teenager.

Doing Things Together

There are many things that you can do together with your teenager involving teamwork or partnership that result in loving fellowship. Pray or meditate together, restore or build something, exercise together, take music or sports lessons, volunteer together, attend or be a helper at your teenager's school play, sport event, recital, or function—the choices are unlimited.

Teaching

Remember when you read stories to your children? Remember when you helped with their spelling words, or taught them to ride bikes or swim? Teaching often goes by the wayside when kids become adolescents. You can teach anything you know that interests your teenager as well. Spending time teaching your teenager how to build a boat, bake, sew, throw a football, or apply a scripture lesson can all be very good ways to express your love to your teenager.

Family Circle

Choose a time when all family members are home and are relaxed. Have a short meeting wherein one person speaks at a time and says positive things about other family members—things they appreciate or wish to praise. This will increase the odds of that person repeating the positive behavior, and it builds family cohesion and togetherness. Doing this while the family is having dinner at the table is a great idea.

Caring Days/Love Days

Choose a day to give your teenager your undivided attention. This is a Valentine's Day for your adolescent. Send him or her a gift or flowers; give extra hugs, kisses, and I-love-you expressions. Do something with your teenager that she especially likes to do. Go fishing, attend a rock concert, go on a hike, ride bikes, go shopping, and so on. Spend the entire day being out and about and listening to her talk and enjoying her company. Rotate the Love Day to include every member of the family.

Thank-You-Grams/Love-Grams

Write notes that you leave out where the teenager will find them—by his bed or on the kitchen table. A written note carries more weight than a quick "thank you" or "I love you, guys" tossed over your shoulder as you run out the door. The thank-you-gram recognizes your teenager for something he has done that has pleased you. The love-gram is an expression of affection and/or recognition. You can combine the two or use one or the other. For example, "I saw how hard you worked on the project today. I just wanted to say I think you're a great kid. I love you. Dad."

Laughter

Humor makes the heart feel light and the day go easier. Share jokes and stories with your teenager. A little gentle teasing can build intimacy and express love. Have some fun with your teenager. Do things together as a family that will induce laughter: watch a silly movie, play a goofy game, have a water balloon or snowball fight. When you can laugh together, your love will shine.

Incentives and the Defiant Teenager

One word of caution: for adolescents who are *heavily involved* with crime, drugs, alcohol, and/or antisocial behavior, reward-based methods will likely prove to be a failure. These kids think they have already have everything as they wish it to be and are being continually reinforced for their behavior. To them, doing drugs, drinking, stealing, assault, vandalism, and cutting school are fun and worthwhile activities. They do not care if you are unhappy with their behavior, and they don't need you to tell them how to live. They certainly don't see any need to "earn" freedom and privileges. They already have them.

Likewise, defiant kids who have weak emotional attachments to their parents may do poorly with a reward-based system. I very strongly urge you to *not* give up on these kids. They can and will respond with due diligence. First, take the five steps of the active consequence (chapter 4) as the first attempt to regain control. Once these antisocial behaviors have been brought under acceptable limits, you can start using reward-based incentives to help maintain the positive behavior.

When used consistently, rewards and incentives are powerful tools in changing the focus and direction of your teenager's behavior from negative to positive—no matter *how* negative the behavior may be. Just as a lathe is a tool used to "shape" material into a desired form, rewards and incentives can help you "shape" your teenager's behavior into the form you want to see. You just need to know how to use the tool properly to make it work for you to get the result you want. And now you do.

PROBLEM BEHAVIORS AND
WHAT TO DO ABOUT THEM

Part II provides suggested rules and consequences for problem behaviors. One or more of these consequences may work consistently
in helping your teenager alter his or her behavior. If the effectiveness of the consequence begins to fade—or is plainly not working with
your child—don't be afraid to try another. You can make a Rules Tracking Guide on which you list the rules, monitor compliance, and record
progress.

The problem behaviors covered in this section are:

Arguing	Sexual Activity
Chore Completion	Sibling Fighting
Driving	Stealing
Drug/Alcohol Use	Swearing
Friends	Television
Information Technology	Tobacco Use
Lying	Truancy
Running Away	Violence
School Assignments/Homework	Whereabouts and Curfew

ARGUING

Sample consequence rule: Never argue, discuss.

Natural consequence: People do not want to be around teenager because he/she is unpleasant, objectionable, and tiresome.

Logical consequence: When your teenager begins to argue, do not talk to him/her and walk away.

Active consequences: Argument deflectors, sponge, broken record, the wall, and clouding (see below for skills).

Parent educator Gregory Bodenhamer asks how many times have you won an argument with another person? How many times has the person suddenly stopped with a look of enlightened astonishment crossing his face and said, "You know, you're right! I never thought of those things. I don't know how I could have been so wrong! I want to thank you for your profound wisdom and for pointing out the error of my ways. From now on I'll always listen to you." Now think, how many times have you won an argument with a teenager? When pigs fly.

Arguments are verbal combat. They are not designed to persuade with reasoned discourse, but rather to wear down an opponent. Arguing is by its very nature harmful and unproductive. It destroys relationships. Even when you think you win, you lose.

You can't win an argument with anyone. You can only engage in one, going around in circles.

Kids see arguments as a wonderful diversion. They may try to get you into an angry argument about what a lousy parent you are: you are so unfair, you never listen to their side of things, you're always picking on them, you never let them have any fun, they're old enough to choose for themselves, and so on. If they are successful in getting your goat they can divert you from the issue at hand and on to something else—often something completely unrelated to the topic at hand.

Here is the key to "winning" an argument with a teenager: never argue. Yeah, but that is easy to say and hard to do, especially when the kid is yelling and in your face. That's right, it is hard to avoid arguing right back and not returning anger with anger. Anger begets anger, and arguing is the blood brother of anger. To learn how to avoid and deflect arguments, you need practice using the right tools.

First, learn to control anger. There are any number of good books on the subject and therapy programs. If you can't control anger you can kiss any hope of avoiding arguments with your teenager goodbye.

Secondly, understand what arguing is: raising your voice; using insults and putdowns; being unwilling to let the other person speak and to listen; and repeating the same words again and again—only louder. Arguing is also denying that what the other person is saying is true or has any merit. Arguing is the absence of reasoned discussion. It is communication with malice.

Do not let your teenager bait you into an argument. Adolescents are frequently masters at throwing out emotional hooks and reeling their parents into an argument. Emotional hooks usually begin with the word "you":

- You never let me do anything!
- You never listen to what I have to say!
- You and Dad are always against me!

Teenagers also employ the insincere question:

- What's the matter, Dad? Don't you trust me?

- Why is it that everything I say and do is wrong?

- Don't you love me?

And the time-honored manipulative con of sidetracking:

- All my friends are doing it! Their parents trust them. They're cool. They don't care how late their kids stay out.

- Well, if I don't get to go, how come I have to keep my room clean?

- If you hadn't married Jim, I wouldn't want to be out late with my friends.

What is the solution? Be prepared for arguments with argument deflectors, a way to short-circuit arguments. You "deflect" the argument buy never letting it start.

Argument Deflectors

There are any number of words or phrases that can be used as argument deflectors. Gregory Bodenhamer suggests the use of the words "regardless" and "nevertheless." If you like a touch of formality, there is "be that as it may," "notwithstanding," "in any event," or "nonetheless." If you wish to address the issue more directly, there is "that is not the point," "even so," "just the same," or "even though you may think/believe otherwise." They work like this:

- Regardless of how late your friends can stay out, be home by curfew.

- Regardless if you believe it's not fair, finish your chores now.

- Nevertheless, you cannot attend an R-rated movie.

- Nevertheless, I need forty-eight hours notice before you can go to a party.

- Be that as it may, the rule stands.

- Even though you may think otherwise, I will never buy you a motorcycle.

The Sponge

The sponge, another technique from Gregory Bodenhamer, unemotionally soaks up the argument with these phrases: "Uh huh"; "I hear you"; "You already said that. Was there anything else?"

The Broken Record

If your adolescent continues to argue after you use the argument deflectors and the sponge, try the broken record. Simply repeat the consequence rule or your brief explanation—not ad nauseam, once or twice should do. What is the last thing that the teenager hears? The rule or the explanation.

- The rule is you'll do all of your chores and homework before going out.
- The rule is attend every class every day school is in session.
- That is against our family values for someone your age.
- I understand you don't like it, and you'll need to baby-sit your brother tonight.

The Wall

Still arguing? Try this exercise. Pick any wall in your house. Pull the blinds so that the neighbors won't see you. Now walk up to the wall and start to argue. Were you able to persuade the wall to give in? To change its mind? I call this technique "the wall." When your teenager continues to argue after you have tried these other skills, use the wall. Simply stand there and say nothing. Retreat into stony silence. Walk away. Lock yourself in the bathroom. Silence makes most people uncomfortable, and it will drive a habitually arguing teenager nuts. It's very effective.

Now, what if you're afraid of the arguing teenager? You've used the wall and locked yourself in the bathroom for five or ten minutes, but you're afraid your teenager will beat on the door, or trash the house. Take a cell phone with you before you go so that you can call for help if things get out of hand.

Clouding

Somewhat related to argument deflectors is clouding. Here you simply agree with some small aspect of what the teenager has said before you dismiss it or totally disagree.

- Yes, I agree we do have strict rules.
- I agree. Your friend's parents give them more freedom.
- That's right. You are not a little kid anymore.

This technique throws the arguing kid off balance. The last thing he expects you to do is to agree with him. He expects you to argue. Instead, you are simply acknowledging the facts: yes, it really is Tuesday, and he has had a week to finish his uncompleted English assignment due tomorrow. You are not arguing about whether or not it's stupid and if he really has to do it.

Yes, I agree that we have strict rules about completing homework assignments before they are due. I agree that your friends' parents give them more freedom about completing assignments and turning them in late, and we do not. That's right, you are not a little kid anymore, and I shouldn't have to remind you, but I do because you are not yet self-directed about doing your homework. You are absolutely right. You can handle it. I shouldn't have to be networking with your teachers—and I will network until you can handle your schoolwork consistently.

Like the others, clouding is a very effective tool to divert arguments.

If They Have a Valid Point

Now what do you do if you would be willing to cut the kid some slack? Maybe they do have a point or you do want to consider at least some of what she wants. First, repeat the rule about never arguing but discussing. This signals to the teenager that you would be willing to seek common ground. Next say, "I am willing to discuss this with you, but I will not argue with you. What would you like to do?"

What if the teenager keeps arguing only because she wants the last word? Kids want the last word as a means of saving face. Let them have it. You have already won the argument by not engaging in it.

What if the teenager has been firing barbed arrows at you and you don't feel like discussing anything with her? In that case, unemotionally ask her about her intentions: "Did you want me to know how you feel about me, or did you want to try and resolve the problem?" You've left the door wide open for the teenager to take the mature stance of engaging in some active problem-solving with you. Or she can continue to berate you and get—nothing

Most kids—just like adults—repeat behavior they think is in their own best interest. When parents use these tools consistently, kids learn very quickly that arguing is not in their own best interest. Then they stop doing it.

Arguing immediately puts you in a one-down position with your teenager. Never argue, and you'll never fear having to confront your teenager.

CHORE COMPLETION

Sample consequence rule: Do all of your assigned chores every day they are assigned.

Natural consequence: Teenager lives in a mess, with the resulting inconvenience and emotional upset.

Logical consequence: Choose any of the following to say to your teenager:

- For every chore of yours that I do, I will charge you a set amount of money.
- For every chore that I do for you, you'll do one for me.
- For every chore that you do not do, I will withhold one favor from you.
- For every chore that you do not do, you'll be assigned another in addition to the uncompleted chore.

Active consequences: Tracking, monitoring, and supervising.

Chores for kids usually fall into one of two categories: things that affect the teenager directly, or things that affect everyone in the family. Ideally, there should be a balance between the two. If everyone eats off the dishes, then everyone should have a turn in washing the dishes. If the teenager has a bedroom to himself, he should be responsible for its upkeep. If everyone uses the bathroom, then everyone should have a turn in scrubbing the toilet; likewise, if the teenager has a bathroom to herself, she needs to get acquainted with the toilet brush.

When your teenager is an adult and working in the "real" world, will he be expected to do only the work that involves him directly, or work that benefits the entire organization? At times it will be both. Chores are good training for the real world. The worker who knows and can perform multiple tasks in the workplace is usually the best worker.

Well, what's wrong with letting the kid be a kid? He'll have plenty of time to take on responsibilities when he becomes an adult. Think for a moment about the most irresponsible adult you know. This person is in and out of jobs, relationships, and trouble. Now think, how good do you think this person was at doing chores as a kid? Not very. And likely even today this person relies upon others to clean up every mess that he leaves. Doing chores as a child gives rise to the responsible adult.

Kids with weak attachments to the family often find that when they are relied upon in a positive way by having chores, their feeling of attachment to the family and their sense of self-worth increase. Attachment also has the side benefit of decreasing resistance to doing chores.

Chores should be necessary, fair and reasonable, clearly understood, and enforceable—just like rules. In fact, you can examine the prospective chore assignment with same perspective you used in constructing rules (chapter 2). It is a good idea to ask each family member which chore—if any—he or she might want to do. Some kids like chopping firewood or dusting the furniture. It is also a good idea to rotate responsibility for chore completion—especially for the most odious chores. The one thing you do not want to do is let the teenager have no chores, or to do it yourself because it is just easier that way. Everybody is somebody, and everybody can contribute.

Once you have settled on the chores you want your teenager to do, the best way to ensure their completion is to have the chores done on a schedule. Just as you brush your teeth in the morning on a regular routine, so should your teenager be expected to complete chores on a regular routine.

A written chore list is better than an oral commitment. It is also a good idea to run through *in detail* what you want your teenager to do and when it is to be done. Show your teenager, "This is what I mean by a 'clean' room; mowing the lawn means thus and so on; preparing dinner involves doing this." This procedure will help prevent arguments and upset feelings later over what standard is being used.

For example, if you want the bathroom cleaned, you might write out the standards like this:

> Before 9:00 am every Saturday morning, clean the entire bathroom. Find the cleansers under the sink. Swish a cap-full of the toilet cleanser into the bowl and then brush the sides, the base, and the rim with the toilet brush until they are spotless. Do the same to the sink and tub with the tub and tile cleanser. Pick up all of the soiled towels and place them in the hamper. Find fresh towels in the closet and put them on the racks. Sweep the floor and empty the trash can.

Natural Consequences

Natural consequences can be used to enforce chore completion. If you don't have to look at a mess, perhaps you can live with it. You can shut the teenager's bedroom door and walk on. For example, on washday when the underwear is still on the bedroom floor—so be it. If the teenager wants clean underwear, she can make other arrangements—or be sure and have them in the hamper on the next washday. No matter how it goes, your teenager is making the choice and has the natural consequence.

Logical Consequences

Logical consequences can be devised for the adolescent to experience and can likewise be used to enforce chore completion. Look for the consequence that is most consistently effective and logically related. Confiscation and taking away favors/privileges are two good logical consequences to use. For example, if the child flatly refuses to keep his room clean, then confiscate the room or objects in the room. Start by removing the bedroom door. If the defiance persists, confiscate items in the room until the teenager decides it is to his advantage to comply with keeping the room clean, or padlock the bedroom for a day or two. He can earn back confiscated items—or use of the bedroom for the day—for every day the room is clean to established standards. Conversely, you can take away

117

privileges or favors until the teenager determines that he can do chores after all.

Active Consequences

Active consequences are the most useful with the semi-responsible and the irresponsible teenager. You will want to employ the active consequences of tracking, monitoring, and supervision. Make sure that you get your teenager started on the chore with clear written instructions, and then track her progress and the chore's completion periodically (every ten minutes or so). Or you may need to provide supervision by being present the entire time the teenager is working.

Timer

For the kid who does the chore but is a real slug, consider using a timer. Have one timer set for her and another one for you (some kids will try to set back time). If your teenager can't finish the chore in a reasonable time, she can have a second chore. However, be sure to praise her for successfully completing the chore on time when that happens, and offer an incentive for consistent success. For example, if she completes the chores well and on time four times in a row, give her a break from doing the chore the fifth time. When you have consistent compliance, move back down to a milder consequence for not completing the chore on time, or none at all.

Working Together

For infrequent work chores, such as cleaning the gutters, planting a vegetable garden, or painting the house, consider making it a family affair with everyone having an assigned task. This practice can help build family cohesion and a sense of identity. Be sure to give clear instructions. Tell the teenager, "If something I said was unclear, be sure and ask again rather than waste your time and effort." This lets your teenager know that you value his time and effort and expect him to accept some of the responsibility for the success of the project.

Sometimes there may be unexpected and unplanned chores that the adolescent could be assigned, such as picking up a relative at the airport, taking the cat to the vet, changing the bag and the filter on the vacuum cleaner, or doing small repairs around the house. Some parents have everyone in the house take a turn at one of the unexpected chores. Circulate a red laminated card with the word "chore" written on it. The card is given to the next person in line for the next unplanned chore. When the chore comes up, it is his or her turn.

Working on Behalf of the Family

It is fine to have chores that are primarily connected to the child's place in the family, such as cleaning their bedrooms, making their beds, taking care of their pets, and taking care of their things. It is also an excellent idea to have them solely responsible for chore completion that affects the entire family.

They can make a monthly budget and pay the bills (with you signing the checks), do meal planning and grocery shopping for the week (with receipts), or make all of the medical and dental appointments for family members (written and verified). You can also have simple, routine chores that everyone does together, such as doing the laundry or making dinner: "Okay, we're having tacos tonight. Jenny, you fry the meat, Mark, you shred the veggies, and Dad and I will make the salsa and drinks and set the table."

Positive Reinforcement

As for "rewards" for routine, expected, and assigned chores, as someone once said, the only reward the child needs is praise for a job well done; good behavior is its own reward. However, especially with difficult and defiant kids, when you are first attempting to establish a new behavior—such as chore completion—it is an excellent idea to include chores in your point system, or to contract for chore completion (see chapter 5). However, the point system/contract for chores works equally well for kids without any history of defiant behavior. When the behavior is ingrained, you can withdraw the points or the incentives in the contract, and usually the new behavior will stay in place. As adults, we perform our chores because our parents or caregivers taught us to do so, and any incentives we may have gotten at the time are long forgotten.

Work for Pay

If you want to teach your kids the work ethic, then hire them to do jobs around the house or in your business in the same fashion that you would hire any worker. Pay at least the minimum wage (or a set amount for the job). Be sure to specify exactly what is to be done, how it is to be done, and when it is to be done. A good way to do this is with an if/then contract. This is a business arrangement between you and your adolescent, so feel free to treat it as such. McDonald's has a six-hundred-page operations manual that specifies in the minutest detail how to do every job in the restaurant. Your teenager should expect no less of a business arrangement from you than he expects from a clown.

CHAPTER ELEVEN
DRIVING

Sample consequence rule:

- Observe all of the traffic laws and rules of the road.
- Follow all of the requirements in the contingency contract.

Natural consequence: Traffic tickets and other legal sanctions; vehicle accidents.

Logical consequence: Loss of the use of the vehicle for a specified period of time.

Active consequences: Networking, monitoring, and tracking.

For most adolescents obtaining a driver's license is akin to obtaining a magic carpet. To paraphrase Dr. Seuss: imagine the places you'll go and the things you'll do!

Teenagers usually think about the power and the freedom that come with driving. Parents think about the privilege and the responsibility—not to mention the expense and the danger, although many kids prove to be excellent drivers.

CHAPTER ELEVEN

Contracts

Adolescents and their parents often have different wants, needs, and expectations about teenager driving. It is important to be clear whose wants, needs, and expectations will be met, and how, before the teenager ever gets behind the wheel. Since written commitments in this regard are far more effective than verbal agreements, I would especially recommend the use of an if/then contract (page 60) for driving.

Driver's Ed

Parents should insist that their adolescent successfully complete a driver's education course, either through the high school or a private agency. Once that is done, kids should be road tested by a responsible adult who you choose to further test their driving skills. Even before they start driving, some parents link together grades, part-time jobs to pay for the car, and driving. Each one is made contingent upon the other, with schoolwork leading the way. If you see a drop in grades, have employment and driving take a backseat until grades are back once again where they should be.

Rules and Guidelines

Once your teenager has earned a driver's license, it is very important for you and she to establish some guidelines related to driving. Some kids will need consequence rules for driving. Without clear rules that are consistently enforced, teenage driving can quickly deteriorate into a motorized nightmare.

If your teenager will be driving the family jalopy along with everyone else, it is important to establish some minimum standards for its use. Issues such as maintenance, fuel, cleanliness, permitting passengers, allowing others to drive, and observing the rules of the road should be considered. Be very specific. If you want the gas tank filled when it gets to a certain level, you need to say so. If you want the oil changed after a certain number of miles and the interior maintained to a certain standard, and if you have requirements about where, when, and under what conditions the car can be driven, you need to be very explicit.

It is a horrifying fact that car crashes are one of the leading causes of death among teenagers. Most kids who are in wrecks are there because of intoxication, excessive speed, or distraction (talking on cell phones, texting, talking to friends). You may need explicit rules and consequences about drinking/drug use, speeding, and paying attention while driving.

If the adolescent will possess her own car, who will pay for it? Who will pay for the insurance, gas, oil, upkeep, repairs, and traffic tickets? Can her friends drive the car? If she totals the car, will you be willing to indulge her with a second car, or will you expect her to learn from the natural consequences? Who gets to decide if this will be a shimmering power machine or dependable, safe, dull transportation?

Some kids—like some adults—kiss their brains goodbye the second they get behind the wheel. Some kids think of their cars as an amusement park ride. Still others think of it as an extension of their bedrooms—they like to eat, work, and recreate in their cars. And if they are not diligent about keeping their rooms clean, image the inside of the car.

Networking

If your teenager thinks he is a drag-strip driver, a Hollywood stuntman, or in a rolling carnival ride, you'll need to monitor his driving closely. But except when you see him driving, how can you stop him from driving like a fool? This is where the skill of networking can prove useful to you. Ask for the network's help in monitoring your teenager's driving. If my teenager is burning rubber while peeling out of the school parking lot, I want to hear about it. If my teenager is seen cruising the main drag in town yelling at people while leaning out the window, I want to be informed. And if he is clocked speeding on the Interstate, please give me a call. Give all of your network contacts the license number of the car and a description of your teenager.

In some communities, parents of driving teenagers have formed networks solely for the purpose of monitoring teenagers' driving. The irresponsible adolescent driver must agree to have a sticker placed on the rear bumper inquiring "How is my teenager's driving?" with an accompanying 800 number to call. Some parents also have the offending teenager pay for the 800 number. You may want to consider establishing such a network in your community. Several Internet companies also provide this service.

Monitoring and Tracking

Further, there are a number of increasingly sophisticated electronic monitoring devices you can have installed on your teenager's car that provide you with a written record—downloaded to your computer—of his or her driving habits: speed, braking, acceleration, and so on. You can track the teenager's car location and location history with installed GPS devices. Suddenly, it seems like everyone and his dog is watching your teenager's driving habits and he can't do anything—except drive safely.

You can also limit teenage driving by time of day and location. The newly licensed driver can only drive the car during daylight hours, cannot drive on the freeway, or can only drive from point A to point B. Some states have such restrictions in place already by issuing provisional driver's licenses. Find out if this is the case in your state.

A less effective, but still good way to monitor your teenager's driving habits is to track her receipts of traffic violations. Establish a logical consequence for each traffic violation. A good one to use is overcorrection, wherein the teenager must drive to perfection for two weeks with Mom, Dad, or another trusted adult sitting next to her.

Logical Consequences

If the teenager has a car of his own, and the car is used as an accessory to a crime—driving while drunk, for example—or if the car was involved in some prohibited behavior, such as permitting friends to drive it, having sex in the car, or driving foolishly, you can put the car on blocks, use a tire boot, install a steering wheel locking device, or take away the keys for a set number of days; the more serious the misbehavior, the longer the restriction. If it continues unabated, then put the car up for sale. If a teenager is involved in repeated instances of drinking and driving, have ignition interlocks installed on the car. A breathalyzer in the dashboard will not allow the car to start if alcohol is detected.

Legal Consequences

The ultimate legal consequence for some adolescents is to lose their license or the right to apply for a license. In some states a teenager will *au-*

tomatically lose his driver's license for possession of alcohol and/or illegal drugs until he is eighteen. Even then, his record will show up when he applies for car insurance, a very expensive mistake. Additionally, in some states you have the legal right to request that the Department of Motor Vehicles rescind your teenager's license.

Driving is a privilege for all of us. Most kids will honor it. Those who don't must learn from the consequences their behavior choices bring. They should have plenty of time to think about that while they are riding the bus.

CHAPTER TWELVE
DRUG AND ALCOHOL USE

Sample consequence rule:

- Never drink alcohol until you are of legal age.
- Never use illegal drugs.
- Never use a drug or a substance for any other reason than for medical purposes.

Natural consequence: Intoxication, sickness, disorientation, impairment of judgment, or death.

Logical consequence: Loss of privileges—driving, attending parties, associating with friends. Grounded to the home. Legal restrictions and consequences.

Active consequences: Intercession, networking, tracking, monitoring, and supervision.

In today's world it is not a matter of *if* your kids will be exposed to pressure and opportunity to use drugs and alcohol, but *when*. When this happens, your teenager will have a response; so should you. Your teenager has seen a thousand beer commercials where everyone is drinking and having a good time. He knows people his own age who like to "party" by using drugs—it must be the thing to do because you can't have a good time without it. Consequently, adolescents often feel tremendous social pressure to drink, smoke, and use. Too many kids believe that using such substances will be a harmless exercise in an altered state of consciousness, not a harmful or fatal exercise in stupidity.

Stages in Drug Use

People proceed through stages in drug/alcohol use. Everyone starts out at the *experimental* stage, the "I-just-want-to-try-this-once" stage. Many kids, with no apparent drug history, graduate to the *occasional* user stage—using on weekends, at hangouts, with friends, and on special occasions. This is the kid who smokes a little weed and drinks a few beers, but only at the party on Friday night. At this stage, some kids become quite skilled at hiding their drug use and you will not necessarily see a drop in grades, friends, and usual activities. Further along still is the teenager at the *regular* user stage. The regular user uses when she can, what she can, and as often as she can and may not be very particular about "what's in it" as long as it gets her high. And finally, the teenager at the *addicted* stage uses not for fun or relaxation while socializing, but because he must in order to just maintain some semblance of his daily life.

Some kids will tell you that they "don't use" when in fact what they mean is that they don't use on a daily basis. Kids that "don't use" and do use substances can die of acute alcohol poisoning, from a drug-induced heart attack or seizure, or from respiratory failure at any time. Dead. Not any consolation to the grieving parents when someone says, "I don't get it. He wasn't a druggie."

Interestingly, no kid ever says, "I want to be a junkie" or "Yeah, man, I want to be an alcoholic—that would be cool." No kid ever says that it would be a wonderful experience to be locked away for months in a rehabilitation center and spend $40,000 of his parent's money to get clean and sober. And yet thousands of kids have the experience every year. It all starts so simply.

Why do they do it? Drug and alcohol experimentation among adolescents is a function of naivety and peer pressure, coupled with curiosity and thrill-seeking, and the sense that it won't hurt to try it at least once. Consequently, many "good" kids as well as kids who have less-than-desirable traits try drugs and alcohol. Further, many "good" kids know the dangers of using drugs like heroin and cocaine and methamphetamine, but could be pressured and talked into using substances that do not appear to be harmful because they are legal. For example, "huffing" involves inhaling the chemical fumes from aerosol cans, gasoline, glue, and the like. Teenagers who try huffing have the sword of Damocles hanging over their head. A teenager (or adult) can easily die or suffer irreversible brain damage the first time he huffs. The same is true with "pharm" parties, where kids take mood- and mind-altering medications from home medicine cabinets (often washed down with alcohol) with the intent of getting high.

Drugs do not care about gender. Drugs do not care what race you are, what religion you practice, or what your educational or economic status might be. Drugs do not care about your loved ones or your dreams. Drugs are an equal opportunity destroyer.

What can parents do?

Networking, Monitoring, and Intercession

Most kids have their first direct exposure not with the local drug dealer or liquor store but with their peers (sometimes also with parents or relatives). Therefore, one important key is to know your child's friends and your child's friend's parents, and what their values are regarding the use of chemicals. Almost without exception, kids try dangerous substances for the first time when they are with someone else, usually a friend who has access. Experts say an adolescent is nine times more likely to use drugs or alcohol if his or her friends do. If you have suspicions about your teenager's friend using drugs, you'll want to monitor what is happening when your teenager is with the friend, and want to network with the parents of that friend.

Many of the same recommendations about being sexually active (see page 161) apply to teenage alcohol and drug use: teach your kids your values, be a responsible model, teach them refusal skills, discuss what they see and hear, gently challenge their thinking, and know whom they are with, where they are, and what they are doing. Knowing these last three things consistently will require constant application throughout adolescence. Your teenagers will remain at risk for the entire time.

If you have evidence your teenager is huffing chemical fumes, for example, educate him on the dangers (see the Internet), remove or secure all items from the house he can use to do it, network with your sources, and then track and monitor what he does outside the home. The same is true for kids who use hallucinogenic drugs such as LSD or ecstasy, marijuana, alcohol, or any other substance of choice your teenager may have access to, including over-the-counter and prescription drugs.

Parties

A massive amount of serious alcohol and drug abuse occurs at parties. There are parties that are not for dancing and socializing, but boozing and stoning. When your teenager gets an invitation to a party—any party—you need to know certain things before giving permission for your teenager to attend. *Who* is hosting the party and *who* are the invited guests? *Where* will the party be held and *what* are the hours? *What* kinds of activities are planned? *Who* is providing responsible adult supervision? And *will* alcohol or drugs be served or allowed? If you hear *yes* to the last question, your answer to your teenager is *no*.

There are a few parents and other adults who will supply alcohol and drugs on the theory that since the kids will do it anyway, why not have them do it in the house where the adults can keep an eye on things? These parents will take the car keys and monitor how much the kids drink. Besides, they want them to know that they're cool. There are a few adults who want your teenager chemically impaired for their own reasons: to sexually molest them, or to get them on the road to addiction and dependency.

Consider the advice: "trust but verify." If you have reason to believe that you may have been deceived about adults providing drugs or alcohol to minors, go to the location of the party and see what your teenager is doing. Alternatively, call the police and tell them where the teenage party is and request that they do a "knock and talk" to see if there is any illegal activity.

Most experts believe that it is best for the teenager to give her parent forty-eight hours' notice if she wants to attend a party where the parent is unsure about the details. If this is a party at the community center, place of worship, school, or the best friend's house, you may only need a few hours' notice because your need to check it out isn't as strong. You can extend the forty-eight hours' notice rule to attending concerts or youth nightclubs.

Supervising Parties

If you are chaperoning a teenage party, supervise both *in* and *out*. Walk through the party once in a while. Have a responsible adult monitor the front door so that kids will not be able to bring substances in to the party, or go out and come back in drunk or drugged.

Safety Plan

Your teenager needs a plan to follow if she finds herself in a situation not of her own choosing in regards to drugs and alcohol. Help her to devise such a plan. Have her carry a cell phone or at least coins for phone calls. If she is at a party and someone has or brings chemicals to use or she finds herself in a car where someone has been or is using, she needs to call for help and to leave the area immediately. Some families devise code phrases teenagers can use when they call their parent: "Uh, Mom, I left my stuff at Bud's house. Can you come pick me up?" If your teenager does make the mistake of using, and she calls you to pick her up, do not impose consequences the first time it happens because you want her to always feel assured about calling for help. Depending on the circumstances, you *may* want to impose consequences the second time—but always do pick her up—otherwise she may come to think of you as a willing cab driver for intoxicated teenagers with no consequences afterward. Tell your teenager with a history of repeated substance abuse beforehand that if she drives her car while drunk or stoned—and manages to escape in one piece—you will put her car up for sale the next day.

Logical Consequences

In many states adolescents can be fined and lose their driver's license until they are eighteen, or lose their right to apply for a license, for the *first* drug/alcohol offense. In some jurisdictions, the adolescent can be cited by police for just *being with* another kid who is using. Further, their car insurance rates will skyrocket. In some communities parents can be held legally accountable for the behavior of their drug-addled kids. Help your teenager develop a plan to avoid such situations before they happen.

Intercession

What do you do if your teenager is already using? You can use the experience of an unpleasant natural consequence coupled with a logical consequence for the novice or infrequent user. For the teenager who is using chemicals regularly, you need to start with the intercession of professional assessment and treatment, and then track, monitor, and supervise his opportunities to use. You can also network with the adults in his life.

Kids who are heavily involved or addicted to drugs/alcohol will need to be thoroughly assessed by professionals and will require professional care to recover. This could mean residential care, or hospital treatment, or wilderness experience programs with intensive aftercare.

It may also mean that after your teenager comes home, you'll have to implement some seemingly radical measures for a time in aftercare yourself, such as confining the teenager to the house at night (with smoke alarms and practiced fire escape procedures in place) away from his drug-abusing friends. I don't recommend locked bedrooms, iron bars, and attack dogs, but you may need to secure the hallway and his bedroom window with motion-detector alarms and the front and back doors with double key dead bolt locks to keep a teenager from cruising the neighborhood with his friends for a hit or a drink. If your teenager is actively using, you will need to search his room, computer, locker, car, backpack, and clothes. *Your right to know supersedes his right to use.*

Tracking and Monitoring

What else can you do? If drug use has escalated to the regular or addicted stage, you must turn up the heat of intervention and prevention to put a stop to it. The key is to acquire information about when and where drug use is taking place, and to supervise and prevent the opportunity to use. With that in mind, there are relatively cheap and effective electronic devices for recording phone calls. Check visited websites and correspondence for drug connections. Miniature cameras can be installed in common areas of the house. There are chemical sprays and wipes to turn up drug reside in cars and on flat surfaces, and products to test someone's breath for alcohol. Home urinalysis kits can be bought in drugstores. And there are Internet companies that test for illicit substances by using a lock of hair, or have drug-sniffing dogs for rent. Some parents have hired private investigators to have their drug-abusing teenagers tailed. Before you take any of these radical steps, check the privacy laws in your area.

Most parents will feel absolutely awful about spying on their teenagers and putting them under surveillance—as well they should. It is a terrible thing to trespass on someone's conversations, correspondence, and behavior. It is a more terrible thing still to watch a kid fall into the pit of addiction and serious harm because of substance abuse. You must weigh your teenager's right to privacy against your need to keep him from harm. You must consider how a temporary rift in trust and relationship could potentially save your child's life. When a teenager is actively using substances, and possibly storing them in the house, most parents would agree that the teenager's right to privacy in using dangerous and illegal substances has come to an end.

Certainly it is far better to talk to your kids early and often about drugs and alcohol, and to confront them directly if they are caught in experimental use. However, if a teenager's use has progressed and gone underground to avoid detection, you must be willing to fight underground to stop it. So when do you stop using these dirty, underhanded tactics? When your teenager stops using for good. For the good of all concerned, you don't stop until then.

Finally, report *anyone*, adult or teenager, whom you have reason to believe, beyond casual suspicion, has supplied your teenager with booze or drugs. How long will you need to do these things? Until your teenager is clean and sober and determined to stay that way.

This kind of close monitoring and supervision will help the kid who wants to say *no* but doesn't want to be embarrassed in front of her friends. She simply tells her friends that Mom and Dad are crazy and will have her busted the minute she hits the door. If she stays clean as a whistle for several months, well and good. She can go to the next party or excursion with her friends.

However, for the adolescent with a repeated history of serious drug/alcohol involvement, don't rely on a single indicator of how she is doing. Use the forty-eight-hour rule, use periodic tracking and networking, and use random drug testing consistently.

Monitor what alcohol you have in the house (if you need to, count the number of bottles of beer you have in the refrigerator) and lock your liquor cabinet. Put any mind-altering medication you may have under lock and key. And, of course, be a responsible role model and never use illegal drugs yourself or permit others in your home to do so.

As the parent, you want to stand between your teenager and a drug habit any way that you can. It is never too early to be concerned, and it is never too late to intervene.

Most kids try alcohol and many kids use illegal or mind-altering drugs at least some time during their adolescence. You may not be able to stop experimentation, but you certainly can help prevent the exploration that leads to a quagmire.

CHAPTER THIRTEEN
FRIENDS

Sample consequence rule:

- Bring all of your friends to the house so I can meet them.
- Bring all of the friends you wish to associate with to the house so I can meet them.
- Always ask permission if you wish to do something with _____.
- Never associate with _____.

Natural consequence: Teenager has experiences with his/her friends.

Logical consequence: Parent restricts or increases contact with the friend based upon teenager's behavior choices.

Active consequences: Intercession, networking, tracking, monitoring, and supervision.

The most common rallying cry of adolescence is: "You can't choose my friends!" That's right, you can't. You can certainly influence and guide your teenager in the choice of friends, but the ultimate choice is the adolescent's. Likewise, the behavior choices your teenager makes while with his friends are his. So are the resulting consequences.

Should we permit our teenager to experience whatever may come with his friend? To a certain extent, yes. Our teenagers need these experiences to understand the intricacies of personal relationships. They will discover for themselves whom they trust and count on, and whom they must steer clear of. For most adolescents, next to their parents and loved ones, their friends are the single most important and influential people in their lives. We should hope that they choose them with care.

Know the Friends

What do you do if you're concerned about your teenager getting into trouble when with his friend? First, start with a reality check. Establish a consequence rule about the need to meet all of your adolescent's friends. (If you can meet the teenager's parents at the same time, so much the better.) Have your teenager write down the name, address, and phone number of each of his friends in an address book He can do this every time he makes a new friend. Carry a list of friends' names, home and e-mail addresses, and phone numbers with you at all times; some parents put the list in their personal electronic devices.

Networking

You want to get to know your teenager's friends—and their parents. Ask them over for dinner or coffee, or meet them at the soccer game, the park, or the mall. But make it a point to meet them. Ask polite and friendly questions. Later, suggest that the kids spend some time at your house. Try to get a sense of what the friends' values are and what they think is important. If they appear to be good kids with good families, you're done.

If a red flag goes up in your head, tell your teenager your concerns. If he wants to continue to see the kid, tell him that you will hold him personally accountable for all of his behavior choices when he is with the friend. If he makes appropriate choices, how long he sees the friend is up to him. If not, restrict him from seeing the friend. The more serious the behavior problem(s), the more serious you'll be about restricting access.

In a very few cases, there may be no access. None. Zip. Zero. These are kids who are enmeshed in crime and violence and who wish to recruit your teenager's participation. How do you stop your teenager's contact with these kids?

Monitoring

Most of these kids are wards of the juvenile court and are on probation or parole. In most states you have the right to find out if a teenager of concern is a ward of the court. If so, request that the court officer inform this teenager that he or she is not to associate with your teenager by making this a condition of the probation/parole. (If your child is on probation or parole, then it's even easier.) If he continues to do so, he will be violating the court's order. The last thing a teenager in the juvenile justice system wants is to be back in court over a matter as seemingly minor as being friends with your kid. There is always some other kid whose parents do not monitor his friendships that he can hook up with. If the teenager is not involved with the court, tell him that you are watching like a hawk and will be on the lookout for *any* illegal activity when your teenager is with him. Tell your teenager the same thing. If that is not working, seek a no contact or restraining order.

Well, won't some teenagers likely sneak around and still see each other? Probably. And won't some kids just flat defy their parent's attempts to restrict access? Could be. And didn't I say earlier that would just make the other kid appear to be more attractive in the eyes of your teenager? I did.

The key is to restrict access *on the parent's terms.* The kids can still talk on the phone, send e-mail, see each other at school, and be at the house together, but because they shoplifted at the store, they can't go shopping together. Because they get in trouble when together, your teenager and his friend can go to the movies together, the football game together, and skateboarding, but only under a parent's or trusted adult's direct supervision for a specified number of days. And your son and his girlfriend are not to be in the house together without a chaperone because they were caught in sexual and drug activity.

Intercession

What if the problem behavior is more serious or continuous? Then your consequences need to be more serious and continuous. Start with intercession. Communicate your specific concerns about the friend using straight talk. If you have a loving relationship with your teenager, it will greatly increase your chances of being heard and heeded.

An easy way to formalize the process is to place your teenager's friends in mental categories. An *A* category teenager is a teenager that you know, a teenager that you trust, and a teenager whose parents you know and trust. Your teenager can do anything within reason with this friend without your needing to be concerned or involved. This should be the majority or all of the friends your child is involved with.

The *B* category kid is one that you don't know. Depending upon how trustworthy your teenager has been in the past when he has been with friends, you *may* need to restrict access on your terms, or until the two kids have a history of satisfactory behavior choices when together.

A *C* category teenager is one that who has a history of unacceptable behavior when she has been with your teenager. When the two kids are together, they require monitoring and supervision, or no contact for a specified period of time.

Finally, a *D* category friend is one who has a criminal, violent, and/ or substance abuse history *and* is seeking to recruit your teenager into the same activity. This friend is not to associate with your teenager. Period. You enforce this restriction by any legal means necessary.

Can kids move from one category to another? Sure they can. It all depends on what your teenager chooses to do when she is with her friend. Further, if an *A* category teenager engages in some serious misbehavior when with your teenager, he or she can move to the *C* category for thirty days, or, alternatively, you can have a no contact period for thirty days.

A word of caution. If you say something like "I know he's involved in using drugs. He's got tattoos and a nose ring," you'll sound ridiculous to your child. Because the kid listens to punk bands, or dresses all in black, or has a foul mouth is not a sure sign of anything, including that your teenager will follow suit.

Need for Belonging

If your teenager does follow along, it most likely means he or she tends to be easily influenced and is hungry for emotional attachments. If your teenager becomes involved in criminal or harmful antisocial activity when with the friend, be ready and be armed. Be ready to restrict, and in some cases completely stop, contact with the negative friend. Be armed with the *facts* of what you know about the friend's behavior and your teenager's behavior when with the friend.

Sometimes your teenager's situation is compounded by entanglement with a negative friend who abuses her: "You don't understand, Dad. He didn't mean to do that. He is not like that; he really loves me." Here your teenager is wading out into swift currents and doesn't even know that she is getting wet.

In addition to restriction, you should seek professional therapeutic help for the teenager who is abused or who is emotionally attached to antisocial friends and can't seem to stop the association. There are better ways to belong.

Monitoring and Networking

What about the adolescent who has "secret" friends—friends whom your teenager never brings to the house and doesn't want you to meet? Here you must carefully and consistently monitor *where* your teenager goes, *whom* he says that he is with, and *what* he says that they are doing. If there is wrongdoing, the secret friend will eventually turn up. If there is no wrongdoing, then your adolescent should have no qualms about introducing his friend. Stipulate that you'll turn down the heat on monitoring their activities when you meet "all" of his friends.

Also, you can ask your network for help. Some people may be able to tell you whom your teenager is hanging out with and what their names and reputations might be: "Well, I don't know if they're friends, but I've seen her hanging out with so and so and this person's reputation is thus and so."

Intercession

Some kids have difficulty making and sustaining friendships. There are very specific things kids can do to make friends, and to avoid getting into trouble when with certain friends. Have your teenager talk to a school counselor or family therapist to learn these skills. Also, encourage your child to move in circles where he is more likely to meet kids with positive attitudes and values—places of worship, volunteer groups, youth camps, activity clubs, sports teams, and the like.

Some adolescents are so unsure of themselves and their lives that they gravitate toward peer groups that seemingly have the answers. Kids in gangs and cults no more have the right plans for your teenager than the serpent did for Eve. Some of these groups have an almost magnetic attraction for some kids because they can provide many of the same characteristics as traditional families.

Peer Influence

A large body of research shows that adolescents vary widely in the extent to which their peers influence their behavior. Studies demonstrate conclusively that adolescents are much more likely to be heavily influenced when the quality of the parent-child relationship is poor, when self-regard is low, when they believe they are frequently criticized and emotionally rejected, and when they believe communication is spotty with little encouragement for positive behavior.

Further, kids who have immature, impulsive, narcissistic, and emotionally unattached personalities are especially likely to be influenced by negative peers and groups. But even these kids don't *run* into delinquency and other problems; they *drift* into them. Refer to "Kids, Gangs, Cults, and Negative Peers" on page 37 for ways to help your teenager resist them.

Adolescents want desperately to fit in and to be accepted by their peers. There is nothing wrong with that. The experiences your teenager has in making and sustaining friendships is the anvil on which adult relationships are hammered out. As parents, we want to be sure that our teenagers can complete the work successfully.

INFORMATION TECHNOLOGY

Sample consequence rule:

- Follow all the rules for using the computer. They are listed under the file name "rules."
- Never post identifying information about yourself to strangers.
- Always guard your password.
- Always ask me for help or permission if you are not sure what to do.

Natural consequence: Having experiences of different kinds on the computer.

Logical consequence: Time restrictions on computer use. Filtering and parental control devices in place.

Active consequences: Intercession, networking, tracking, monitoring, and supervision.

M y ten-year-old daughter knows more about using her computer than I do mine. In the twenty-first century, teenagers' lives will be evermore intertwined with their personal computer, especially with the Internet. Rather than going off to search the world, the Internet brings the world to them. There are many wonderful things on the Internet for kids to learn, see, and do. Unfortunately, the Internet also has nests of vipers that parents must guard against. They crawl into our home through the portal of cyberspace.

If your teenager surfs the Internet, makes social contacts, and uses the computer in responsible and trustworthy ways consistently, then let them continue to do so. You only need to establish some reasonable guidelines and rules.

Restrict Personal Information

Think about the social networking sites your teenager may be involved with. Most kids post personal profiles, photographs, messages, and even names, addresses, and phone numbers for all the world to see to attract attention and new friends—often without their parent's knowledge. Revealing too much personal information not only is incredibly dangerous, but also can be perused by prospective employers, college admissions boards, and criminals for years to come. If your teenager has a social network website, you'll need to establish rules for its use.

Dealing with Exploitation

Think about the people your teenager will come into contact with while online. Consider using the same mental categories for people your teenager has contact with on the Internet that you have in the three-dimensional world:

A category: a person you know and trust
B category: a person you don't know
C category: a person who has gotten into trouble with your teenager through computer contacts.
D category: a person who has solicited or engaged in criminal behavior with your teenager as a result of computer contacts.

An *A* category person may have unsupervised contact with your teenager. A *B* category person you need more information about. A *C* category person has no computer contact with your adolescent for thirty days, or your teenager has a thirty-day computer restriction. A *D* category person

141

has no contact whatsoever with your child, and you file a police report about the wrongdoing.

The U.S. Department of Justice reports that one in five teenagers is known to receive adult sexual solicitations online. Most of these adults lie about who they are, their age, and what they want from the child, although many pedophiles are brazen about stating their age and intention. Have a rule that you are to be told immediately if anyone asks for personal information or a meeting—regardless of how old that person claims to be, or benign their stated intentions.

If your teenager is in the habit of posting inappropriate content on his or her web page, or accepts solicitations from strangers, tell your teenager he or she must post a prominently displayed statement on the web page that says, in essence: "I am fourteen years old and this is a monitored website."

Tracking

When exploiters or predators see such a message, they will move on to hunt for easier prey. If your teenager refuses to post the message, block all access to the computer until they do. Then go online periodically to check the website for content and the posted message. Also, periodically scan the Internet for images and information about your child that may have been downloaded by others for their own purposes.

If you need to play it safe, then do so. Educate your teenager about the dangers of the Internet. Install and use filtering and parental control devices. Block everything that is not pre-approved or is not under the heading of approved guidelines. Limit engagement with chat rooms to those that are monitored, or ones that contain "safe" topics. Locate the computer in a family area of your home where you can supervise its use. Network with the school, the public library, and your child's friends' parents about computer use in their location or home.

If your teenager has a cell phone, pager, or other electronic device, understand its capability to download images and software and to receive and send text messages. Use the same safety measures with the device that you have in place for the computer. Some cell phone companies set limits on minutes and messages, send family priority messages, and control the time of day and day of the week the phone can be used. These steps will not ensure your teenager's safe journey in cyberspace, but they will make it much more likely that your teenager will not drive off a cliff.

Preventative Supervision

Finally, if (or when) your teenager is trustworthy with computer use, establish a twenty-four-hour rule. Tell your teenager you trust that he or she is making good decisions when online (the vast majority of kids do) *and* you will continue to monitor the computer. This is what you can say:

1. I respect your privacy.

2. In twenty-four hours I will go online to your website or blog to check for content.

3. You have twenty-four hours to remove anything that is inappropriate or store anything that you do not wish me to see or to read.

Information technology is here to stay. Like fire, it is a wondrous tool that has transformed the human condition. And like our ancestors, we want to make sure that our children do not fall into the fire pit.

CHAPTER FIFTEEN
LYING

Sample consequence rule:

- Never lie.
- Always tell the truth.
- Always tell me the whole truth when I ask you about something.

Natural consequence: People do not believe what the teenager says. People question what he/she says. People do not trust him/her. Teenager has a reputation as a liar.

Logical consequences: Every time the teenager lies, he/she needs to make restitution by apology, payment, or service.

Active consequences: Networking, intercession.

All children lie at some time, beginning at an early age. Sometimes the lie is not intentional, but is based on fantasy. Later on, around the age of four, children learn to lie to try and avoid embarrassment or punishment. And sometimes, just like adults, kids lie to gain something that they want. When a teenager lies, he typically lies for the same reasons. Usually, however, he is more adept at lying than is a young child because he has had more experience. And, of course, some older kids never lie.

Natural and Logical Consequences

If an adolescent lies rarely or infrequently, which is the case with most kids, it is best to let the teenager experience the natural consequence of lying or the lie. The essence of the logical consequence for lying is to make restitution. The adolescent needs to make a formal apology to the person or place that was lied to. Or he needs to make payment by losing a privilege that is logically related. For example, your teenager lied about his whereabouts—he said that he was going over to Bob's house to study, but went to the mall to meet Sally—he should be restricted from going out for few days, and in having contact with Sally. As a result of his lying, he will now have the experience of losing your trust for a while. He can try again in a few days to begin earning trust once again.

Networking

If an adolescent is lying frequently, use the active consequence consistently. The art of lying has practical value to the teenager only when he can *pass* the lie. If he knows that you will verify every lie, or potential lie, lying will quickly lose its practical value and effectiveness. Ask the network to contact you if anyone thinks your teenager is lying. Your adolescent will quickly learn that lying is counterproductive and can lead to the very embarrassment and consequences that he was trying to avoid by lying in the first place.

Truth-Telling

Further, you can greatly increase your odds of the teenager giving up lying by doing two things. The first is to praise your child consistently when you have certain knowledge that they are telling you the truth when you have asked them about something. Second, use the point system (chapter 5) to target lying as a behavior you want to see less of, and truth-telling as a behavior you want to see more of.

Going to the Source

Even when they know the truth, some parents like to question their teenager in hopes of "catching" them in the act of lying. It is pointless to ask the kid with orange teeth if they ate all of the Cheetos. This practice usually only encourages teenagers to continue to lie in order to support the first lie.

If you're not sure if this is a lie, check it out every time. You do this by *going to the source*. Check directly with teacher, the neighbor, the friend's parents, and so on to get their version of what transpired.

Training a Child Not to Lie

You can also directly train your teenager not to lie. Give the teenager with a history of lying a chance to clarify seemingly conflicting facts or statements by using the "you said A, she said B" procedure.

> Your teacher said that she counted you absent, that you did not come in late. You said that you got to class after attendance was taken. Now before I impose a consequence for lying, which one of you is correct, or did I misunderstand what you said?

A second training method is to tell your teenager "this is the truth as I know it to be."

> Doug, this is the truth as I know it to be. I know that you didn't go to three of your classes today. What I don't know is where you went when you cut class. Now before you have a consequence for lying, would you care to tell me where you were?

Your teenager now has a chance to back out of the lie, before a double consequence is imposed (one for lying, one for the misbehavior), and he can still save face. Like politicians who are caught in a lie, they didn't really "lie"—they "misspoke." Fine, let's have the truth now.

If you're still not sure of the truth you can say, "I will check it out; my information is different." Then go back to the source and check it out.

If you have suspicion, but no evidence of wrongdoing, you can say "I believe" followed by an inquiry:

"I believe that the car has been driven. Do you know anything about that?"

"I believe that money has been taken from my purse. What can you tell me about that?"

Intercession

If an adolescent is lying habitually, it usually means something else is going on besides lying. She is engaging in a variety of undesirable or forbidden behaviors that she wants to cover up, or there is an emotional problem that needs to be addressed in counseling. Either way, be ready to intercede with available help.

CHAPTER SIXTEEN
RUNNING AWAY

Sample consequence rule:

- Never run away from home.
- Never leave home without parental permission.

Natural consequence: Teenager will be tired, hungry, cold, lonely, and at risk for harm.

Logical consequence: For every hour teenager is gone from home without permission, he/she will be grounded to the house for three hours. Teenager will be given a small amount of freedom out of the house with frequent check-ins, for several weeks.

Active consequences: Networking, tracking.

Most teenagers run away from home some time. It could be to the end of the street, or to a friend's house for a few hours. Usually it is because the teenager is upset and needs some space. Sometimes kids run off for longer periods of time and to less-than-desirable people and places.

Parent educators frequently make the important distinction between *running off* and *running away*. Running off is taking a time-out without notifying anyone as to where you are. Running away is leaving home for indefinite periods of time without parental notification or permission.

Although some kids wouldn't even consider it to be "running away" when they are gone overnight, give your teenager with a history of running these definitions.

Teach kids that when they are so angry or upset they need to leave the house, they must tell you where they are going and when they will be back. If this is a safe place—Grandma's house, down to the park in daylight hours, sitting in their car—let them go. It's not okay to be angry and jump in the car and go barreling down the highway, hang out at the bus depot, or go over to the home of forty-year-old neighbor "Uncle" Stan, the convicted child molester.

The vast majority of kids who run—including kids who run habitually—run to their friends. Most never leave town. Some friends will sneak the runaway food, clothes, or money or have them sleep in the house after everyone else has gone to bed. The teenager may also move around from friend to friend and location to location, especially if they think you and the police are actively looking for them.

Abuse in the Home

There is only one legitimate reason for teenagers to run away from home: because of abuse. So what do you do if a teenager is legitimately running away from home because of physical, sexual, or neglect abuse, and you are aware of it? There are four things to do:

1. The non-abusing parent needs to immediately find a safe place for the teenager to stay.

2. The non-abusing parent needs to practice intercession for the adolescent: police reports, no contact orders for the abusing parent or family member, legal advice, and so on.

3. The abuser needs to be out of the home before the teenager comes back.

4. Arrangement for the teenager to see a therapist who specializes in abuse issues.

As for the non-abused teenager who runs away, most such adolescents engage in "magical thinking" about life on the run: no more school, no more rules to follow, doing exactly what they want, whenever they want. Jobs and money and good times will flow easily their way. But life on the run rarely works out that way. You will not locate your child lazily floating down the river with Huck Finn.

Hazards of Running Away

The supposedly tranquil waters of freedom are full of riptides. Streets and neighborhoods are rife with adults who dress like sheep and behave like wolves. When a teenager is on the streets for any length of time he or she runs the risks of the natural consequences of being tired, hungry, cold, and lonely, as well as the distinct risks of being beaten, robbed, raped, and murdered. Charismatic criminals, gangs, cults, drug addiction, prostitution, and sexually transmitted and bacterial diseases can also ensnare teenagers. Some runaway kids evolve into homeless kids, living in parks, shelters, and "couch surfing" with friends and associates. Some also trade sex for money, drugs, shelter, or protection. There are teenagers who are spirited away by adults and are never seen again. Can such things happen to teenagers where you live? They can and they do.

Rules at Home

What if your teenager will not follow the rules at home? Shouldn't he be kicked out of the house until he can come back with assurances that he will follow rules? This "tough love" approach is somewhat akin to the school practice of expelling students for nonattendance. There is nothing logical about it. Where do we want the teenager to obey the rules? At home. How can they learn to follow rules when they are not there? It is better to keep teenagers at home and consistently apply the consequence that goes with the rule. It is tougher and more loving than giving them the boot.

Invitations to Run Away

Some parents quite inadvertently invite their teenager to run away: "If you think you're living with Mr. and Mrs. Tyrant, don't let the door hit you in the butt on the way out, pal." Some kids deliberately misinterpret these kinds of phrases said in anger and haste as meaning that they are *kicked* out of the house. And, of course, there are a very few parents who will not tolerate a child's living at home or return. Such kids are called "throwaways." In this instance, sometimes it is the *parent's* issue: parents who are addicted to drugs or alcohol, domestic violence, criminal conduct, poverty, and mental illness can all contribute to an intolerable situation. If you have any experiences like these in your home, don't give up hope and seeking help for change.

If both you and the teenager need some time away from each other, make it for a specified number of days at a safe home or youth shelter of which you approve. Work on the problems you have together with your teenager by appointment and in a neutral setting while he is staying elsewhere. See chapters 6 and 7 for communication and problem-solving skills you may be able to use. Seek a family therapist or professional mediator to help you find common ground.

Runaway Prevention

There are things to look for *before* your teenager runs away. If the teenager is thinking or planning to run away they may become moody and secretive (even more so than usual). He may withdraw from social contacts and refuse to discuss what he is thinking and feeling. He may make vague references about how things will be "different" around here soon enough.

Make it a habit to talk to people in your network about things they may have seen or heard in regards to your child. Walk through your neighborhood periodically so that you can have an idea who and what is there; this is important because most kids run to their friends, and some never leave the neighborhood.

Some teenagers plan their escape like prisoners of war. They slowly withdraw cash from bank accounts, make contacts for help online, horde food and other supplies, and keep a backpack of clothes in the closet for when the time is just right. If you see evidence of this behavior, it is time to have a talk with your teenager.

Getting Your Teenager Back Home

What should you do if you believe an adult is harboring your child? Such an adult can be charged with custodial interference and contributing to the delinquency of a minor when that adult is having or has had your teenager in his or her home without your express permission. Parent educator Gregory Bodenhamer suggests sending a registered letter to the suspected adult who is providing haven for your teenager. Tell that person that if your teenager shows up at the door without your prior approval, he or she is to send the teenager home immediately. Tell them what the consequences will be if they decide to harbor the adolescent without your consent. Let them know that a copy of the letter will be forwarded to the police. The next time your teenager runs to that home, the adult stands a good chance of going to the county jail. Chances have improved dramatically that they will tell your kid to go home, which is exactly what we want.

Other tips are, if you do not have it, install caller ID on your phone, so that when your runaway adolescent calls, but will not divulge her location, you can have the number traced or recorded. Conversely, after she returns, you may have her carry a pager, or GPS device (personal locater) with a cell phone for a while so that you can have her "check in" when called to do so. You can make it a rule: "When I call you, call me back within five minutes."

Keep a personal log of bits of information and clues as you search for and track your teenager. If you have the resources to do so, you may want to hire a private detective to track the adolescent. If you cannot afford that, become your own gumshoe, including staking out locations where you think the teenager may be hiding. Use a rented or borrowed car to avoid easy detection. Don't forget to check in with frequent hangouts that your teenager likes: the video arcade, the pizza place, the skate park, and the mall. Talk to anyone—especially kids—who may have recently seen your teenager.

Networking and More Things To Do

Talk to your teenager's friends and ask them what they know. You think your teenager's friends won't tell you anything? You're right, they won't— if they don't know you, don't trust you, don't think your teenager is in danger, or don't care about your teenager. So you want to get to know and cultivate a positive relationship with your teenager's friends *before* your kid runs away. Why? Kids usually tell their friends they're thinking of doing something they shouldn't before they actually do it, such as having sex for the first time, using drugs, attempting suicide, or running away. If you have developed a positive relationship with your child's friends (and their parents), it can be of tremendous value to you when your teenager has left home. Also, when you call friend's parents you may find out that their kid is missing as well. The kids could be together.

You never know what information may prove useful to you or to the police. When you call the police to report your teenager as a runaway, be sure to obtain the police report number for future reference. Ask the police to "stand by" if you find your runaway teenager and they refuse to come home without a fight.

Alert the network—the adults in your teenager's life—that you are looking for the teenager and would like their help. Many teenagers visit school to see their friends. Ask the school to notify you the minute your child is seen on campus. Take a recent photograph of your child with a written description and have a printer make up flyers for you. Post the flyers all over town. Many kids will come home just to get these "wanted posters" taken down.

If you teenager has a bank account, call the bank and have the funds frozen. Store all of the teenager's clothes and lock up easily obtainable food items in the house. Without easily obtainable money, clothes, and food, your teenager is more likely to come home quickly.

Dealing with Habitual Runaways

For the habitual runaway, confiscate all of the possessions he or she has left behind—phone, computer, TV, makeup, jewelry, stereo, CDs—and store them in a safe place outside the home. When your teenager returns home, she can earn each item back, one item per day that she completes with verified check-ins and appropriate behavior. She should also complete the six-day level system. If she chooses to run away again, escalate the confiscation by placing a padlock on her room. Have her sleep in another area of the house (such as in a sleeping bag at the foot of your bed). She can then only have access to her room for short periods of time while she completes the six-day level system again. A third runaway and the teenager needs to not be allowed out of the house unless it is under strict supervision, and must participate in mediation to recover her privileges.

In my experience, it rarely gets to this level, but if it does, be consistent in following through.

Most runaways return home within forty-eight hours. However, kids who run away habitually often increase their time away the more often they run. If your teenager is gone longer than two days, check with local and national runaway shelters and hotlines (these should be listed in the phone book). Most runaway shelters try to facilitate a return home. Some runaway hotlines allow you and your teenager to post confidential messages for one another.

Tracking

If your teenager is gone more than two days, and you have no leads as to his whereabouts, check out any electronic records that might provide you clues as to movement: track phone bills, e-mail and pager records, visited websites, bank accounts, credit card receipts, and bus, rail, or airline dockets. Installed GPS devices on the teenager's cell phone or car can be used to track whereabouts. This is especially useful information if you have reason to believe that your teenager has run away with (or to) an adult. Online sex predators seek teenagers in chat rooms and through social networking websites, and sometimes can lure kids away, often to distant locations.

Finally, when your teenager does come home, if she makes threats to run away again at the first opportunity, confiscate every pair of shoes she owns. When in the house she is shoeless. Limit (or forbid) e-mails, phone calls, and text messages. But more important, actively problem-solve with your adolescent and be loving and forgiving. Many kids who run want to come back home but are afraid of being shunned and shamed when they do

Do these things and your child will learn that running is not a viable option when they see that the parent is running ahead of them. It is better to stay home and work things out.

CHAPTER SEVENTEEN
SCHOOL ASSIGNMENTS AND HOMEWORK

Sample consequence rule:

- Complete all of your assignments before they are due.
- Turn in all of your completed assignments when they are due.
- Complete all of your homework every night it is assigned.
- Complete all school projects before they are due.

Natural consequence: Teenager fails the subject or the grade.

Logical consequence: Teenager studies at home for a set period of time until the teacher verifies that he/she is completely caught up.

Active consequences: Tracking, monitoring, supervision, networking, and intercession.

Most teenagers want to be successful in school. Teenagers spend so much of their lives in school they want to be able to feel that it is a good place to be. As parents, we want them to feel that way about school as well.

Adolescents who do not do well in school usually start going off the track in the late elementary grades or junior high school. This is often when parents start losing track of what is happening with the child in school. It is often not that the parent doesn't care; it's just that the child now has more difficult work to do, has several teachers, and doesn't talk about school as much as he used to.

Some kids become distracted by adolescent issues, family problems, or the influence of negative peers. Still others get drawn into crime, delinquency, substance abuse, or antisocial activities that take them away from school. Some parents believe it's the school's responsibility to educate the teenager and that they are just doing a lousy job of it. Perhaps so. Regardless if the teenager is enrolled in a "lousy" school or not, you can help your teenager be consistently successful in school.

Some parent educators and some teachers believe kids should be allowed to experience the natural consequences of failing the subject or grade. Teenagers should have the "freedom to fail" because they'll learn to do better next time. This belief puts the teenager at risk for harm and is ill conceived. The freedom to fail philosophy teaches a child only one thing: how to fail. We want to teach our children how to succeed.

Logical Consequences

Using a logical consequence is more productive. When you see the progress report or report card that shows your teenager failing one or more classes, you know that he is having difficulty not only in class, but also in completing homework.

Help or direct your teenager to set up a study time and place at home to complete daily assignments, homework, and longer-term projects. Make sure this is a place with plenty of space, light, and quiet. The kitchen or dining room table may be an ideal location after meal preparation and eating are over. To begin with it is usually best to have the adolescent devote a "small" amount of time to schoolwork. Help your teenager be consistently successful with fifteen or twenty minutes of study time a day and then within two weeks increase the time to a half-hour, then forty-five minutes, an hour, and then as much time as is needed (the time begins after she has returned from the bathroom and sharpened all of her pencils). If she has more schoolwork than can be completed in fifteen minutes, have her work in fifteen-minute increments with a five-minute break.

Intercession

If you only know that the teenager is failing one or more classes, but you don't know why, intercede by pinpointing the reason(s). Is he not paying attention in class? Goofing off in class? Not even in class? Is he not turning in the assigned work, failing exams, or not participating in class? Is it that he seemingly cannot do the work? Certainly you want to network with his teachers and school counselor, but you can also find out a good deal of what you need to know to answer these questions by using the School Behavior Checklist provided on the website.

If he seems to struggle with the subject, assist your teenager with tutoring and guidance. Check to see if his school offers tutoring help before, during, or after the school day. There are also a number of reputable tutoring business services and those available online. Also, many schools have adult mentors who can be a source of great help. Find out what your child's school has to offer.

For kids who are actively resisting doing even a short period of schoolwork, hire a friendly gorilla to sit with them and to "help" them get started. Review their assignments with them before they turn them in to the teacher.

Tracking and Networking

If these interventions are not helping to raise your teenager's grades, consider using a Daily Class Assignment Report, on which each teacher signs to indicate that your child attended class, behaved appropriately, completed classwork, and turned in homework, until grades improve. Your teenager needs to bring the report home each day with the signature of each teacher. This strategy strengthens the network and the connection with the school as a whole. Some parents will need a "signature list" of all of the teachers, just to be sure that their teenager isn't engaged in a little creative writing: "Sorry son, no sale; this doesn't even look close to Mr. Johnson's signature." You can also do random phone checks about the assignments, and in many cases communicate with teachers through e-mail and fax. If you think your teenager may intercept written messages or grade reports, have these sent to the neighbor's house or to a post office box. Ask teachers and others to report to you any improvements that your teenager is making. This process will encourage teachers to praise your teenager, which in turn will up the odds for continued improvement.

If your adolescent balks at the idea of carrying the Daily Class Assignment Report, give him the option of your going to school with him a half hour before school starts and talking to each of his teachers. Tell him that you will be happy to do this every time you need to in order to know how he is doing in class. Suddenly, carrying the assignment report won't look so bad.

If your teenager "forgets" to bring home the Daily Class Assignment Report, or she left it on the bus, in her locker, at Roy's house, and so on, accompany her while she retrieves it. Some parents have the school fax them the daily report. If the reason is "the teacher wouldn't sign it," go with your kid the next school day and talk to the teacher and request that they sign it. Have the adolescent carry the daily report until grades and behavior improve, then a weekly report, and finally a monthly report. When all is as it should be, throw the assignment sheets away.

Yeah, but what if one or more of the kid's teachers won't cooperate? Then you talk to the principal. The easiest way for the principal to handle the situation is to direct the teacher to take ten seconds of her time to review and sign the form. No luck with the principal? Talk to the superintendent, the school board, and on up the chain of command until someone realizes you mean business and resolves the issue in your favor. Extending the concept of the Daily Class Assignment Report, many secondary schools now have websites that record your teenager's school assignments and completed work. Your child's record can be accessed via a personal code and is updated daily, so that you can use the DCAR and the website in tandem.

More Intercession

Active intercession can also be useful in more ways as well. In addition to tutoring help, consider enrolling the teenager in reading dynamic, study skills, computer literacy, and memory improvement classes and workshops. In addition, there are many useful videos and computer programs that teach math and reading skills, as well as those that teach science, social studies, art, music, and other subjects. Some kids have great success organizing and tracking their schoolwork with a PDA (Personal Data Assistant), a thumb drive, or other electronic device. Make a point of seeking out teachers for your teenager who demand excellence, especially in such critical areas as math and language arts.

On days when your teenager does not have any homework, you may want to have them stay in the homework routine. Have him or her do a half-hour of reading of good literature of their choice (not a paperback with a bronzed hunk or naked nymphs on the cover), or a half-hour of learning a new skill on the computer (not a game) or solving a math puzzle (at their level). Anything that will exercise the brain muscle in a positive way is useful.

If the teachers think your teenager may have a learning disability, have him tested. The adolescent may also be tested to find out what his predominant learning "style" may be. Some kids are primarily "visual" learners, some are "auditory" learners, and some are "tactile" learners, meaning the teenager may learn best by seeing, hearing, or touching learning material. Learning that takes place in the teenager's dominant style can be much easier and more productive. Some kids, too, may have attention deficit or attention deficit/hyperactivity disorder that has not been detected and may need to be assessed.

Extracurricular Activities

Encourage your teenager to become active in school-related activities, such as sports teams, drama, band or orchestra, choir, clubs, volunteer activities, student newspaper or yearbook, or student government. Some kids do better in school when they have an after-school job. If keeping the job is made a condition of maintaining success in school the job can be a motivator to maintain passing grades and regular attendance.

The reason for your encouragement is because one or more of these positive activities will increase your teenager's attachments to the school. Adolescents who have such attachments usually do better academically, have higher self-regard, and have fewer behavior problems while at school.

Alternative Sources of Education

If your teenager struggles with "traditional" schooling, or is behind in credits, inquire if your teenager's school offers viable alternatives for earning credit: alternative school, night school, summer school, community college classes, work experience programs, credit-by-examination, public television courses, and courses offered through the Internet. Nowadays anyone who wants an education can get one. Ignorance is not bliss—it's only ignorance.

Reinforcers for Success

Finally, offer frequent praise, acknowledgment, rewards, and encouragement for your teenager's effort and successes (see chapter 8). Use of the point system and contracting are two excellent ways to encourage school success. The child will do better next semester *and* the next day. Every teenager can be successful in school. As parents, we can help them build ladders to reach for the stars.

SEXUAL ACTIVITY

Sample consequence rule: Never engage in sexual relations with anyone until you are of legal age and can decide for yourself.

Natural consequence: Teenager runs the risk of pregnancy, sexually transmitted diseases, and emotional confusion and upset.

Logical consequence: Parent teaches teenager about sexual expression.

Active consequences: Intercession, monitoring, supervision.

To be human is to be sexual. Having sexual thoughts and feelings during adolescence is as natural as the sun rising in the morning.

Sixty percent or more of teenagers become sexually active during their adolescence. The kids who do not usually lack opportunity, or have strong internal controls based on religious, moral, or family values about the propriety of premarital sex. Some kids are also afraid of pregnancy, sexually transmitted diseases, and AIDS.

If you do not want your kids to become sexually active, and wish to deter sexual activity, is there anything you can do? You bet.

Teaching

Teach your kids about sex. Regardless of your feelings about sex education in the schools, our kids need to learn about sex at home. I am not suggesting that you tell your kids about your sex life. Nor am I suggesting that you talk about the mechanics of sex.

Adolescents need to know about *sexual expression.* If you believe sex should be a natural element of a loving, committed relationship between consenting adults, and what that entails (such as marriage), tell your kids that clearly and forthrightly. You can supplement your message with material from books and videos that agree with your belief system. Most of these materials emphasize abstinence until marriage or until maturity is reached. The virtues and the benefits of abstinence cannot be overemphasized, but research shows that teaching teenagers about contraception is equally important.

Further, teenagers who are emotionally close to their parents are more likely to remain abstinent than those who are not. If you are not close to your teenager, and you are concerned about their sexual activity, now is the time to get close. Kids who have emotionally close relationships with their parents have what is called *psychological presence.* That is, the child tends to think about what the parent would want them to do when the parent is not with them. When faced with sexual choices, psychological presence can help the teenager make the right choice.

Along with teaching about sexual expression, teach your child your *family values* about sex. Have frank discussions about why you believe what you do. Don't assume that they know—that they've picked it up in church, overhearing adult conversations, or watching TV. If you're not sure what you believe yourself, now is the time to clarify your thinking. Tell your teenager flat out, "This is what I/we believe about people having sex. . . ." When asked, many sexually active teenagers say that they are unsure or have no idea what their parents think about them having sex.

Our teenagers will follow the example of our behavior. Regardless if you want to be a role model or not, our kids monitor what we do and what we say. Parents who are sexually responsible *tend* to have kids who are likewise; the reverse is also true.

Also, just like us, our teenagers are not required to have sex. Telling them to "just say no" is woefully inadequate. Teach your teenager how to assertively, but calmly, refuse a request to have sex. Teach them how to use assertiveness techniques such as clouding, argument deflectors, script technique, and straight talk. You may also want to have your teenager be taught about date rape and self-defense techniques to prevent it.

Monitoring

Be mindful, also, of the sexual predators of both genders who will be happy to supply your child with attention, affection, alcohol, drugs, money, gifts, and promises in order to get him or her to have sex. In some cases you'll need to monitor your teenager's new "friends" very closely, and teach your teenager how to discern if someone is out to take advantage of him or her. This is especially true if the friend is an adult. If you think your adolescent is sexually active with an adult (anyone over eighteen), you may want to file a police report and/or seek a restraining or no contact order against this adult having contact with your teenager.

Discuss with your teenager what they see on TV and in films, read in print, and what they hear in songs and from their friends. Most people do not fall into bed with strangers—except in fantasy—which is mostly what our teenagers are seeing and hearing. And despite what our kids may be lead to believe in certain street culture music and movies, women are not "sluts" and "bitches" who enjoy rape.

Gently challenge teenagers' thinking and expectations about sex. Question these assumptions: everyone does it when they get to be a certain age; it makes your relationship stronger; you need to because you're in love; it always feels good; it's just a part of growing up; all my friends will think I'm a "geek" if I don't; nowadays it's just a part of dating; it's what "real" men do; I can't possibly wait; it's safe.

Explore the last one especially. There is no such thing as safe sex. There is only safer sex. Condoms and other contraception devices are designed to prevent pregnancy and the transmission of sexual diseases. They are not foolproof and are not designed to prevent people from having sex with all its consequences.

Intercession

So, okay. What if your adolescent is already sexually active? Should you teach him or her about "safer sex" and make certain that your teenager has and uses contraception, hoping for the best? You certainly can. Some parents do and leave it at that. Some parents really don't care if their teenager chooses to become sexually active, or think they are powerless to stop it, and a few parents don't care if their teenager is sexually active, even if the result is children born to children out of wedlock.

If you do not pay close attention, you may deeply regret it, especially if you become grandparents before it's time, or know the heartbreak of having a son or daughter who is HIV positive. Reality is that nowadays there are students at your child's school who are sexually active and who are positive for sexually transmitted diseases, and don't know it—including the virus that causes AIDS. Some of these kids do not know that they have the virus, and probably won't know until they are older and begin to show symptoms.

Some teenagers have difficulty understanding the possible ramifications of having sex. If your teenager has not already done so, have him or her spend some time caring for a baby. Let him or her experience the romance of a loaded diaper and the incessant crying of an infant with an earache. Being a single teenage parent is almost inevitably a one-way ticket to poverty and loss of personal freedom. Further, because of its emotional intensity, having sex at a young age can cause heartbreak and ruin a deep-seated friendship. In short, there are a number of very good reasons for your child to abstain from sex.

The Challenge

It is not true that there is nothing you can do to prevent your teenager from becoming sexually active, or continuing to be so. It is true that—short of marooning your kid at the North Pole—you cannot stop him or her from experimenting with sex if your teenager so chooses. Enforcing a consequence rule about sex is difficult. It is not impossible.

You *can* make it more *difficult* for your adolescent to have sex—and thus cultivate the habit. You can monitor his time, activities, and whereabouts. You can supervise when, where, with whom, and under what circumstances he or she is permitted to date or be alone with a girlfriend or boyfriend. You can discourage (or forbid) early and steady dating, or dating others outside of the same age range as your teenager as these kinds of relationships increase the likelihood of your teenager having sex.

Until when? Until you're reasonably sure that your teenager is making responsible choices about having sex. The incentive for the sexually responsible teenager is that he or she can continue to date or be in relationships without close monitoring.

Teenagers with strong values and strong behavioral controls don't have sex. Teenagers with strong values and behavioral controls do have sex. And teenagers who have neither have or do not have sex too. Emphasizing family values and imposing behavioral controls will not stop your teenager from having sexual thoughts and feelings—they may still choose to act on those stirrings. What values and controls will do is make it much tougher to have sex, and make you psychologically present in your teenager's mind when he is making the decision about sex. It can help him make the right decision for now and for his future.

CHAPTER NINETEEN
SIBLING FIGHTING

Sample consequence rule:

- Never put each other down.
- Never say or do anything to be deliberately unkind or to hurt one another.
- Always seek to settle your differences between yourselves before involving one of your parents.

Natural consequence: Parent "divorces" him/herself from teenager's sibling conflicts.

Logical consequence: Parent applies conflict resolution and problem-solving skills.

Active consequences: Intervention.

Sibling conflicts are perfectly normal and to be expected. As children get older, sibling conflicts should decrease. If an adolescent is still squabbling frequently with his brother or sister, you should intervene. Intervening can range from refusing to intercede to settling disputes to everyone's satisfaction.

When children get into a scrap about something, they often seek to involve the parent. How often have you heard the ear-splitting call of "Mom!!!!" or "Dad!!!!" when an argument or tussle is going on between your kids? Each wants you to use your authority on his or her behalf. Your kids are not asking you to walk into a dispute, and using your Solomon-like wisdom, render a just and reasonable solution. No, they want you to hammer the other kid. Each kid is betting that you will err on the side of justice and be on his or her side.

What would happen if you removed that parental power leverage? Why, our kids would be forced to resolve their own problems. What a concept!

When your teenager becomes an adult, who will mediate her disputes with the neighbor? With the boss or the coworker? With her spouse? Does she expect you to jump in the car and go right over to fix everything for her? Not hardly, as the kids would say. Would you want to? Not hardly. Therefore teaching teenagers how to settle their disputes with their sibling should provide good practice for when they have disputes with other adults later on. Still, you could choose to jump in with both feet to resolve your teenagers' disputes for them, unless you have a more pleasant activity planned—such as a root canal—but you would be handicapping your children into thinking that might equals right.

Sibling Fighting

Brothers and sisters often fight about peculiar things.

- "Now . . . I told you to quit breathing my air. Now I'm mad."

- "Mom! Mom! He just snapped my bra and told me to go bite a mailman."

- "You're stupid"
  "Oh, yeah? You're more stupid."
  "Well, you're stupid and none of my friends like you."
  "That's because all your friends are stupid."
  "Dad! Dad! He's calling me names."
  "I'm not! Dad, I didn't say anything, and she started it."

- "You can't sit there. I need that chair for my books."

- "Bolivia exports tin."
  "It does not!"

"'Fraid so!"

"'Fraid not!"

"Mom, Bolivia exports tin, doesn't it?"

And so on. These kinds of disputes are engaged in mainly for their entertainment value. When such hassles develop between kids, it is generally best to not get involved. Do you really care if Bolivia exports tin? Neither do your kids. The argument is simply jockeying for position, in this case which child knows the most about Bolivia.

Sometimes two siblings fight about things as well as ideas: who can use the computer, wear each other's clothes, be in the other's bedroom, what TV show or movie to watch. But do you really want to mediate a war for the umpteenth time over whether they watch a rerun of *Star Trek* or cartoon shows on a cable channel?

Intercession and Consequences

When the bickering starts to escalate into loud voices and putdowns, parents should intercede. (If one kid is soaking the other's kid's head in a bucket of ice water, go ahead and intercede here too.) Restate the consequence rule(s) about sibling fighting. Resist the temptation to get into a referee, prosecutor, defense attorney, or judge's role. Tell the siblings to immediately stop the quarreling and to not start again—ever. If the quarrel does start up again, *immediately* impose a logical or active consequence. Don't threaten, just do it. For example, if they can't be in the same room together peacefully, should they be in the same room? No. Send one to the bathroom and one to the garage. If they need something to do while they are marooned there, have them clean it (some parents have exceptionally clean bathrooms and garages). If you're in the car, pull over to the side of the road until things calm down (although this intervention works better if you're driving to Disneyland rather than the dentist). Here the consequence (such as the work detail) comes about when you return home. The same is true if you are out in the community somewhere; alternatively, whether in or out of the house and the kids start a ruckus, use confiscation or forfeiture.

If they are in the house, when can they come out of timeout/isolation and be together again? When they can do so peacefully. But how will you know that they can?

Problem-Solving

Teach brothers and sisters exactly how to resolve conflicts and actively solve problems by teaching them the skills in chapter 7, "Conflict Resolution with Teenagers." This intervention works well because when people are forced to find a solution to a common problem, they tend to find common ground. As a result they learn to see their sibling not as an enemy but as an ally.

When a brawl starts, interrupt and immediately have the kids begin using the skills. Tell them you'll be waiting for their decision, and will be interested in how it turns out. If they resist, impose a consequence, and insist that they try again.

For example, you've told the kids to decide between themselves which TV show to watch and when—you'll be back in five minutes for their answer. Five minutes go by and they are still arguing. Kiss the TV time goodbye. After an hour of silence, they will try again. This is sometimes referred to as "military justice." Either everyone learns to cooperate and solve problems rapidly, or everyone faces the same consequence. Tough and fair.

Now to be fair, it is a good idea to meet with each child separately *after* the squabble is over so that you can find out what happened and to prevent one teenager from bullying the other. If you know beyond a doubt that one kid was the victim and the other the offender, you can return to the offender and say, "This is the truth as I know it to be," and then follow through accordingly with any additional consequences.

These techniques are very effective tools to compel people to solve disputes. Suddenly, the kids are in a life raft and they must now head toward the shore or sink. The kids will learn very quickly that it is not a good idea to have a knife fight in a rubber raft. Teenagers learn very quickly to row.

Rewarding Positive Behavior

One last thing about sibling fighting. You will increase your odds of success in eliminating sibling fighting by using rewards to deter it. Parents can use the point system by awarding each sibling points for the day for choosing *not* to get into hassles with each other to the point that the parents become involved. I would especially recommend the use of the "unconditional" reward. When you take notice of your kids observing the rules about sibling fighting—and they are being cooperative, helpful, and pleasant to one another—give them an unplanned and unexpected reward. Along with the other skills described above, it will help greatly in siblings learning to be brothers and sisters, and you'll have peace and quiet. Peace and quiet enough for the kids to search the encyclopedia about Bolivian exports.

CHAPTER TWENTY
STEALING

Sample consequence rule:

- Never steal.
- Never take anything that doesn't belong to you.
- Always pay for every item.
- Always get permission to take someone else's things.

Natural consequence: People will not trust teenager not to steal. Teenager will have a reputation as a thief.

Logical consequence: Teenager must pay restitution for stolen items. Teenager may be arrested and charged with theft.

Active consequences: Intercession, networking, tracking, monitoring, supervision, and level system.

Teenagers take things that don't belong to them for one obvious reason: they want it (or think that they do) and stealing is the way to get it. Stealing can also be a means to an end: money for drugs, activities, or things to buy. Stealing is much like lying in that stealing is only of practical value to the teenager if he can get away with it consistently. Conversely, the natural, logical, and active consequences for stealing work much as they do for lying. In fact, lying and stealing often go hand-in-hand. If you see evidence of one, you may need to track for evidence of the other.

If you want stealing to cease, you need a zero-tolerance policy toward stealing in any form. This is simply one offense that you will not tolerate. You must reject any teenage rationalizations for stealing: "everybody does it"; "it's just a little item"; "the stores can afford it"; "they'll never miss it"; "I 'found' it"; "so and so 'gave' it to me"; or "and I suppose you don't cheat on your taxes?"

Logical Consequences

If your teenager steals, do not shame, discuss, or moralize about stealing—he already knows it's wrong. When an adolescent is caught stealing, the best logical consequence is to have him pay restitution. This could involve returning the item or money with an apology, paying the costs to the victim in the form of a refund, or, when these are not possible, working for the costs of the item(s) and donating the money to charity. If the adolescent is arrested and becomes involved with the juvenile authorities, their consequences should be implemented hand-in-hand with yours.

Other consequences for stealing can be loss of privileges for the day on which the stealing occurred, with only basic privileges for the following weekend. If your teenager is already on restriction or a level system (chapter 5) then use the restitution approach in addition to the loss of freedom. If the stealing is significant in terms of value, use the six-day level system.

Active Consequences

For the habitual thief, these consequences will typically have little practical effect for very long. Chances are good that you'll need to implement all five of the active consequences to deter stealing. Start with telling the young thief that only the adults in her life—parents, teachers, and the like—will be permitted to be the judges of what is stealing. They may label an act as stealing by witnessing it, having it reported to them, or by noting that something is missing. Nor can the teenager "borrow" or "use" someone else's things. If she doesn't want to be accused of stealing, then her behavior needs to be above reproach.

Intercession

You may also want to consider enrolling your teenager in a therapy program for habitual stealers (check with your county's adolescent mental health agencies or on the Internet), or have her see a private therapist. Most teenagers who steal are not calculating safe crackers, and most thieves aren't very good at it. Kids who steal frequently do so on an impulse. Counseling programs can teach kids how to resist the impulse.

Networking

Networking with the adults in your child's life is critical. It is much harder to steal when someone is looking over your shoulder. Also, do not leave items that can be carried off easily—such as cash, cigarettes, jewelry, alcohol, and car keys—unattended in the home or with your personal things. You will only fuel the stealing habit. Request that members of the network be mindful of these same things when the teenager is with them.

Tracking

Consistently track what your teenager has possession of and if he has a receipt for each item. If he cannot produce a receipt for the item(s), it goes back where it came from, or when that is not possible, it is donated to charity. In some cases you can advertise a possession—such as the new just-her-size leather boots that she "found" in a box in a field—until you locate the rightful owner.

Monitoring and Supervision

Monitor or supervise the teenager's opportunities to steal. For example, do not permit your teenager to shop in stores unless he is under eyeball supervision. Stealing not only goes along with unsupervised time and situations, but also with *wandering*. Teenagers who steal habitually wander about town, school, and the neighborhood. They also strive to get just as much time away from adult supervision as they can. Put the brakes on wondering by monitoring consistently. Know the basics: whom they are with, where they are, and what they are doing.

Rewarding Positive Behavior and Overcorrection

We want to reward the positive opposite behavior of stealing—which is, of course, not stealing. Use overcorrection to "practice" not stealing in given situations. For example, going to the grocery store without taking things, paying for them, and coming home with correct change and the items that you sent them for. Do praise your teenager when they bring you receipts, and there are no reports or suspicion of stealing. You can also use the point system or contracts to provide formal rewards. Instead of Johnny stealing money to buy a new skateboard, he can in time earn the money by not stealing, and have the freedom to spend all day Saturday at the skate park with his friends. It is easy for any kid to see which is the better choice.

As stealing behavior starts to decrease (and it will with consistent application of these skills) you will be able to restore or extend more freedom to your adolescent as well. Your teenager can be successful at any number of things. Stealing is just not one of them. Stealing may occur no matter how many possessions he has, how much money he may have, how much he knows better, or how much he is loved. But it will stop if you follow through consistently to make it so.

CHAPTER TWENTY-ONE

SWEARING

Sample consequence rule:

- Never swear.
- Never use foul, crude, dirty, vulgar, or obscene language.
- Never use foul or abusive language that is directed at someone else.

Natural consequence: Teenager experiences unpleasant interactions with people as a result of swearing.

Logical consequence: Parent walks away from the teenager when he/she swears or uses abusive language. Parent ignores the swearing. Reponse cost.

Active consequences: Confiscation, argument deflectors (see "Arguing"), networking, modeling, and intercession.

Most people swear out of either habit or anger. Teenagers swear for these two reasons and to establish a position with their parents—that they can shock them, defy them, can't be controlled by them, or that they are really an adult and can swear if they want to.

Salty language has lost its saltiness. From the outhouse to the White House, swearing has become commonplace, and, for the most part, socially acceptable. People don't swoon any longer when they hear a child swearing. In many minds, it's okay.

Given this, and if swearing is commonplace in your home, it will be tough to enforce a consequence rule for the use of bad language. If you or others do it, why can't they? The answer may be because it is not desirable, morally acceptable, or permissible for children to engage in this behavior. Or you may decide that in the overall scheme of things, concern about your teenager using foul language is a low priority. If you do think it is important, is there anything you can do? But of course.

Natural Consequences

The natural consequence is to permit the teenager to experience the disapproval and anger of people who are offended at his offensive language and to let him deal with these people on his own. This intervention is usually only effective with kids who swear infrequently, or who spend a lot of time around saints.

The second most common advice from parent educators for dealing with swearing is two-fold: walk away from the child when he swears or ignore the behavior. (Most parent educators don't recommend washing mouths out with soap, as this is viewed as a relic of nineteenth-century grandmothers.) Walking away from a swearing teenager is a good idea—especially if he is swearing for your listening pleasure. However, this intervention only works if the kid *wants* you to be with him. If he doesn't, and he swears to get you to walk away, then he has developed a handy tool to control your whereabouts. Ignoring swearing usually only works for very young children. Adolescents are wise to you when you ignore them.

Response Cost

Some years ago an American army intelligence officer was serving in Vietnam. He was upset because his troops were bringing him enemy prisoners who had been beaten. He told his men that for every prisoner found to have bruises, he would subtract one day from the soldiers' rest and relaxation time, and he would add one day for every prisoner who had no marks. The colonel started getting prisoners who were—as one soldier told me—"showered, shaved, and dressed in tuxedos." Psychologists call this behavior modification technique "response cost." For every "wrong" response you make, you lose; for every "right" response, you win. This is probably the single most effective technique to deter adolescent swearing, and to encourage its opposite.

These penalties can take a number of forms: losing money, time, privileges, or favors. Some parents have subtracted money from a teenager's allowance for swearing, and have donated the money to charity in the child's name. Some parents have used short groundings, work details, or taking away privileges as forfeiture for swearing or using abusive language, with apologies as needed. I think the single best use of response cost is the losing of favors.

Most parents gladly do many favors for their kids: drive them to the mall or to their friends' house, provide money for entertainment, do chores and run errands, and so forth. You can tell your teenager: "If you do not do what I want, I will not do what you want. If you choose not to follow the rule about swearing by swearing, I will subtract one favor I do for you from a list of favors."

This technique works equally well for teenagers in the habit of swearing at you, the parent. It also is very effective if the teenager uses backtalk, or says something to you that is insulting or insolent. (Of course, it doesn't work in the *least* if you are modeling the behavior of swearing at the child, or saying things to *them* that are insulting or insolent.)

When swearing occurs do not count the number of words, count the incident; otherwise you could wind up in absurdity.

"Let's see, that was five *`#^@! and four *^&%$."
"No, Dad, I said four {#$^* and five ><&%$."
"Oh, right, thanks dear."

Intercession

Other techniques that might prove to be of value include some intercession skills. Just as you have taught them manners, teach your teenager that some people do not like or are offended by crude language. Your teenager may not think it is offensive, but others do. Further, some people will think your kid is ignorant and rude and not worthy of their time and attention because of swearing. This reaction could be especially costly if it is someone your teenager wants to impress—that cute girl in math class perhaps, or a perspective mentor or employer. Tell your teenager too that no one outside of a small circle of dunces will think he is cool, sophisticated, or smart because he can swear. Any fool can do it—and frequently does.

Your teenager says, "Okay, I can't swear, so what I'm I supposed to do when I'm mad?" One father I know taught his children to use alternative swearing: God *bless*; that's *bovine excrement!*; this is all *mucked up*; and the like. As silly as this sounds it worked wonders for that family. Further, it serves to illustrate the stupidity of being unable to speak the language without swearing.

A more practical suggestion may be to take your teenager to a therapist or a counselor experienced in habit and anger control so that he or she can learn the skills necessary to eliminate a ridiculous habit, and to refrain from getting angry without cause. Swearing is a learned behavior and a habit. What is learned can be unlearned, and a habit, any habit, can be reversed in about three weeks.

Praise and Rewards

Like any number of behaviors you want to pinpoint and target for change, you can take notice and praise your child for not swearing in instances when she has typically done so. You can also use the point system to reward her for holding her tongue by not swearing, backtalking, or saying something nasty to someone.

Modeling

When children are young, parents frequently attempt to curtail their own swearing around their children for fear that they'll "pick it up" and embarrass their parents. Why stop exercising restraint when your children become teenagers? Model the behavior that you want to see repeated and don't swear around your kids. This will be hard for some of us—myself included—but it certainly can be done. By listening to their parents swear, kids learn that it's okay to swear—not that it's right or preferable to do, but that it's okay—Dad does it, so does Mom, it's not that big a deal. Further, if you have strong moral or religious convictions about swearing, then your teenager needs to hear that as well.

More Consequences

If swearing is accompanied by arguing turn aside his rants by using argument deflectors and clouding. If the loss of favors used in response cost is ineffective, use confiscation or forfeiture to help him get a handle on swearing. Network with all of the adults in your teenager's life to get reports about swearing when he is not with you. Won't that become absurd? Yes, it will. And when your teenager gets tired of swearing and being penalized for it, he will give it up.

The end result of these interventions is that when your teenager isn't overtaken by anger and frustration and habit, he can be a calm, cool cat who doesn't swear because there is no need for it. This will impress people far more than all the obscenities a kid could recite in a month of Sundays.

CHAPTER TWENTY-TWO

TELEVISION

Sample consequence rule:

- Only watch programs that you have permission to watch.
- Complete all of your chores and homework before watching TV.
- Never watch _____.

Natural consequence: Teenager may be adversely influenced by the content of the program he/she is watching.

Logical consequence: Parent limits the number of hours of TV teenager can watch. Parent restricts access to certain television programs.

Active consequences: Networking, monitoring, supervision.

Television programs exist to sell products. We all know that. In order to sell us products television writers and producers must produce programs that hold our interest. That is why there is so much violence, sex, and lurid detail on television—it holds our interest. It holds our children's interest, too. The average teenager watches three hours of television every day.

There are no research studies that positively prove kids are more likely to become violent, sexual, or salacious because of exposure to TV programs. And there are no research studies that positively prove that they are not, too. Certainly, both teenagers and adults are influenced by what they see on TV; otherwise, advertising would be pointless. Exactly to what extent people are prone to imitate what they see on the screen, no one knows for sure. It is very difficult to show a direct cause-and-effect relationship in correlation studies, especially with kids. If you really don't care what your adolescent wants to watch on TV, or if you're satisfied that your teenager consistently makes good choices about what to watch on TV, then don't make TV an issue. If you do want to limit your teenager's television choices, what can you do? Quite a lot, actually.

Intercession

Some parents make a habit of allowing their adolescents to watch certain shows but consistently discuss the content of the shows with them. You may want to explain that, yes, everyone on this soap opera has premarital, extramarital, between marital, and no marital sex, but this is fantasy, pure and simple. Most people do not behave this way.

Explain further that the values presented in what the characters do and how they treat each other reflect the writer's, producer's, and performer's values. If it is the case, point out that these are *your* family values about sexual and ethical behavior. The same goes for violent content. Squealing tires, blazing guns, flying fists, and exploding debris—along with sexual gymnastics—are plot devices that are cheap substitutes for the effort of presenting real human drama.

Keep in mind that the producers, writers, performers, and advertisers don't give a flip about your teenager's moral development or the content of their character. In response to criticism, they say that is the parent's job; their job is to entertain and make money. They are right. It is the parent's job to teach our children well.

Monitoring

What can you do then if you do not want your teenager watching vulgar comedians, heads being bashed in with metal chairs, mayhem and blood splattering, or cross-dressing skinheads who love Elvis on talk shows?

You can go through the TV guide and mark the shows that your teenager is permitted to watch—which is the honor system. You can monitor and supervise what and when they watch by watching with him or her. You can program, or have your TV programmed to block offensive content, pay-per-view, or adult channels and the like, if you wish. All newer TVs have the "V" microchip that can be easily programmed to prevent your kids from watching certain shows during unsupervised hours. There are devices that only allow a TV to be operated during certain hours. Some parents have locked up the TV in the closet during unsupervised times, or disabled the TV during these times; a few parents have given the TV the boot.

If your teenager is fortunate enough to have a TV of their own in their bedroom, don't forget to use the "V" chip in that TV as well. However, you should encourage your teenager to watch TV with the family at least some of the time. If a kid spends all of their free time alone in their room with electronic gadgets, they are in danger of developing emotional attachments with the TV and other machines that can substitute for emotional attachments with family.

Networking

Well, what if your kids will just skip over to a friend's house or the neighbor's to watch the forbidden program there? Network with adults in that home. Explain that your teenager does not have permission to watch certain programs and ask for their cooperation. Most adults will be glad to give it.

Goodbye TV

Actively seek to get the kids habituated off TV. Limit the number of hours and programs the kids can watch each day. Provide stimulating conversation, books to read, plays to see, concerts and recitals to attend, exhibits to tour, activities to engage in, sports and games to play, places to go, and people to see instead.

If you need to, include rewards for non-TV time in the point system. A teenager who has never been can earn points for attending a play, or for reading a classic novel. They may like it so much that you can discontinue the point system quickly, as TV becomes a lost interest.

The TV pipeline can provide many wonderful programs to enlighten and entertain. It can also operate as an open sewer. We must use our discretion and good sense in helping teenagers become discriminating viewers.

CHAPTER TWENTY-THREE
TOBACCO USE

Sample consequence rule:

- Never smoke cigarettes.
- Never use tobacco products.
- Never use tobacco products until you are of legal age and can decide for yourself.

Natural consequence: Teenager suffers physical and psychological addiction. Teenager acquires diseases that are associated with smoking and using tobacco.

Logical consequence: Parent confiscates tobacco and all material used in smoking.

Active consequences: Intercession, networking, tracking, monitoring, supervision, modeling, and intercession.

Advertising says people who smoke are mature, independent, sophisticated, and are having a heck of a time while doing it. They're cool. You want to be cool, don't you? Why not smoke?

Most children who start smoking do so around age twelve. Seven in ten teenage smokers are still smoking five years after they start. If an individual hasn't started smoking by the age of twenty-three, chances are very good that he or she never will.

Chances are also good that your teenager is quite familiar with the dangers of smoking. However, her frame of reference is her peers. She won't know any fifteen-year-old kids who have lung cancer, heart disease, and emphysema that can be traced back to smoking. She likely will not see anyone in her age group going through the agony of smoking cessation. That's for "old" people, and she is going to live forever. Besides, she can quit any time she wants with the snap of her fingers.

Smoking cigarettes is a *gateway drug* to the use of other drugs. More than 85 percent of kids who experiment with other drugs started with cigarettes. Smoking is also a *gateway behavior* to adolescent antisocial behavior. Teenagers who engage in antisocial behavior often begin by smoking.

As a psychologist, I've had parents tell me: "Look, do you realize how hard it is just to get her to maintain in school and keep her room clean?"; "If she wants to smoke, then smoke"; "As long as he doesn't smoke in the house or around me, I can live with it"; "Hey, I can't very well tell the kids that they can't smoke when I smoke myself"; "At least he's not doing meth or drinking booze"; "All her friends smoke, I don't want her to lose her friends"; "It's just a phase, Doctor, she'll be over it soon enough; what is there to worry about?" Fine. For these parents I would advise not to make smoking an issue.

Intercession

For parents who will make smoking and using tobacco products an issue, I make the following declaration: *Yes You Can.* You can keep your teenager from starting tobacco use and you can get him to stop if he has started. Begin with intercession. If you have good communication established with your teenager, explain explicitly why you do not want him to use tobacco, why it is against your family values for someone his age, and why smoking will lead to serious problems, including the slavery of addiction. Tell him that you love him and only want the best for him. Tell him that it is a fact that eight out of ten adult smokers would like to quit if only they could.

You can use emotion or a dash of humor to get your point across. Tell him about the loved one that would give his heart and soul not to be addicted, or the loved one who gave her life for it. Try explaining smoking this way: "You're going to roll up a ball of dried weed into paper, stick it in your face, set fire to it, and then breathe in the smoke. On top of it, you'll pay dearly for the privilege." Tell your teenager about how his clothes, hair, and breath will stink and his fingertips turn an oily brown; how he will learn to "do anything" for a cigarette, including spending his last dime; and how people will shun him and think he is an idiot.

If it is clear that the teenager is addicted to tobacco, and wants to give it up, then consider medically supervised smoking cessation classes and treatment options. These will be different than those for adults, but they can be found (check the Internet).

Tracking

You can use tracking with the active adolescent smoker. Tracking is simply looking for the tobacco—the bedroom, the car, the backpack, his clothes, school locker, hidden in the sock drawer—and confiscating and destroying it when you do find it as a consequence of rule enforcement (if he was holding it for a friend, the friend now knows not to use him as a storage unit).

If your teenager persists in using tobacco, you can increase the intensity of the consequence. You'll confiscate not only the tobacco, but also the Joe Camel leather jacket, the cool sunglasses, and the fancy lighter she had when she was caught. In those rare instances when they still persist, confiscate and then use forfeiture for the items. She can "earn" the appropriate forfeited items back as rewards in the point system, in this case for the positive opposite of non-smoking behavior.

Legal Consequences

In some jurisdictions, teenagers can be fined for possession of tobacco. Find out if this the case in your community. Tell your smoking teenager that you'll notify the police if she possesses tobacco, and she will be paying the fine. If such a law doesn't exist in your area, request lawmakers enact such legislation. Further, petition that cigarette vending machines be removed from business locations where minors can congregate unsupervised.

Networking

Networking means getting reports of smoking behavior when your teenager is not with you. If he is seen smoking at Greg's house, he won't be going to Greg's house for a while, and network with Greg's parents and all other parents and adults in your network to get reports of tobacco use. Further, you can band with other parents to find out who in your community is making illegal tobacco sales to minors. Which stores and sales personnel are involved? Take a recent photograph of your child into that establishment and tell the manager that you do not want your child to be sold any tobacco products. If you don't get satisfaction, tell the police. Tell the same thing to any adults or the teenager's friends who you suspect are furnishing your teenager with tobacco.

Monitoring and Supervision

Monitoring and supervision involve knowing where the teenager is, whom they are with, and what they are doing. Tell your persistently smoking teenager, "If I can't trust you not to smoke when you're out of the house, then either you'll stay home or I'll go with you." One or two times of "Hi everybody! Yeah, I'm Dana's dad. I'm here to make sure she doesn't light up" will be more than enough to persuade the most ardent smoker to give it up.

Rewards

In my experience, rewards can be very effective in deterring tobacco use for kids. Use contracting or the point system for rewarding non-smoking behavior. However, because tobacco use can be harder to detect than drug use, be sure to track and monitor evidence of tobacco use hand-in-hand with the application of rewards.

As is the case with drug experimentation, you may not be able to keep your kids from trying cigarettes or chewing tobacco, but you can certainly make it much more difficult to cultivate the habit. With consistency, in the majority of cases, you can stop a tobacco-using teenager from continuing. Isn't that cool?

CHAPTER TWENTY-FOUR
TRUANCY

Sample consequence rule:

- Attend every class that you are enrolled in every day school is in session.
- Stay in class for the entire class session.

Natural consequence: Teenager fails the subject or the grade because of missing too many classes.

Logical consequence: Teenager studies at home during free time for the number of hours skipped. Teenager attends make-up classes at school (Saturday school).

Active consequences: Networking, supervision, shadowing, Forfeiture Day.

Playing hooky is a time-honored tradition in American education. Almost all kids skip a class or a day once in a while. That doesn't make the practice right, just commonplace. If your teenager is habitually truant, you'll need to use a consequence rule with a set consequence.

Logical and Active Consequences

The natural consequence is of no value to the truant adolescent. All it does is let him fail. The logical consequences of studying at home for the number of hours missed, or attending make up classes, are very valuable because they teach the importance of time and responsibility. Some schools have in-school detention, after-school class, or Saturday school for truants and late attendees. If so, a boring Saturday school or three-to-five after-school detention can deter many truants.

Shadowing involves going to school with your teenager: escorting the habitual truant to each class, sitting with the misbehaving student in class, and following him or her around school by going to the lunchroom and riding the bus with him or her if need be. Shadowing is an overcorrection technique—attending and performing in class until they have it right. The active consequence of shadowing for truancy is very effective—no teenager wants their mom or dad walking him from class to class or sitting with him in class—but should be used as the *last* consequence. It gives you a place to go if the logical consequence is disregarded. The shadowing technique also works well to deter the teenager who plays the brat, the buffoon, or the bully while at school. Rarely will you need to do this more than *once*.

What if you can't go to school or your teenager actively rebels? Consider hiring a *friendly gorilla* to accompany your teenager to school, sit with your teenager in class, and in the lunchroom, and accompany him to the bathroom (same-sex gorilla, of course). Or maybe the gorilla rides the school bus home with your teenager and sits with him while he does his homework at the kitchen table. You can also network with other parents to hire an "on call" gorilla—such as a parent volunteer, or you can enlist the help of a relative or family friend for this task.

If you cannot find anyone to help you, consider hiring an escort service for the day (not that kind of escort service). There are professional youth escort services whose job it is to transport unwilling kids to psychiatric hospitals and treatment centers. For a fee they may be willing to consider escorting your teenager to all of his classes.

Also, see if you can enlist the support of a vice principal, the police liaison officer at your teenager's school, or the school's security team to help you track and monitor your teenager's activities and whereabouts during the school day. Ask if one of them could escort your teenager to class.

What if your teenager just shoots out the back door or refuses to go to school the next day after period cuts? Tell her that you'll be back until the day of shadowing is completed. What if your teenager says that they'll be glad to have you come to class the next day? She will not be so glad when she sees and hears the reaction of her classmates.

Forfeiture Day

As an alternative to shadowing, you can use what I call Forfeiture Day. The next available free day the teenager has from school is forfeited. The teenager spends the equivalent number of hours or days that he was truant completing work projects on his day off (without compensation). You can also arrange that he do a half-day of schoolwork (Saturday school at home) and a half-day of labor. Activities such as pulling weeds, cleaning the oven, and scrubbing the floors and toilets should do nicely.

Another alternative is to take your teenager to work with you (or send him to work with a trustworthy adult) and have him sit for the day. There is no reading (other than schoolwork), TV, music, games, phone calls, text messaging, conversation, or other forms of engagement—he just sits where you can keep an eye on him and reads his social studies text and does algebra problems.

Networking

Establish a personal network with someone in the school administration whom you can talk to on an as-needed basis. You want to be made aware of even one class cut *every time* it occurs. Ask for a same-day telephone call with the information that you need—which period or periods were skipped, and if the teenager was seen in other locations. If a teacher sent the teenager out of the room, find out why. What if you think the teenager will intercept the call on your voicemail or dispose of any mailed written messages? What if you can't be called at work? Ask a friend or relative to take the calls for you or to receive written notices from the school. You can also use a post office box, cell phone, fax, text, or e-mail messages.

Rewards

It is easy to pinpoint the behavior that you want to see changed. It is in the sample consequence rules. Tell your teenager that you will use any of these techniques to stop truancy. Also, they can avoid the negative consequences *and* earn positive rewards for the positive behavior of regular school attendance through contracting or the point system.

Intercession

What if your adolescent refuses to attend school because of an emotional problem, an issue with a teacher, they are being harassed, bullied, or threatened, or the inability to do the work? What if they are involved in antisocial activity? Find out precisely what the problem is and then provide the necessary intervention.

What if she says, "School is boring and all the teachers are a bunch of jerks; besides, you don't pass if you attend class and do the work 'cause it depends on if they like you or not"? Such claims are an invitation to dance—the dance of arguing. When your teenager starts singing this tune—don't dance. Instead, deflect the argument (see "Arguing") and then help her get ready for school.

CHAPTER TWENTY-FIVE
VIOLENCE

Sample consequence rule:

- Never hit or deliberately injure anyone.
- Never use or possess street weapons.
- Follow all laws in regards to weapons and violence.

Natural consequence: Arrest or citation by the police or school authorities. Bodily injury, maiming, or death.

Logical consequence: Legal sanctions; confiscation and forfeiture.

Active consequences: Intercession, networking, tracking, monitoring, supervision.

Violence was the most pervasive scourge of life in the twentieth century. More blood was needlessly drawn in that century than any preceding one. Let us hope that the twenty-first century will be better. Some people say that the violence seen in regional wars and in the world at large, the community, the media, and our homes is simply a reflection of living in violent times. Perhaps so.

Regardless of the origin or cause of interpersonal violence, we as parents are not helpless in deterring and stopping our adolescents from engaging in violence. You need not be a prisoner of doubt and fear—fear of your teenager, or fear of what he or she might do to others.

If an adolescent is continually engaging in violence, he certainly will experience one or all of the natural consequences listed above. After a time or two, some kids will throw down the sword on their own accord—if they live that long. This is customarily a kid who engages in less lethal forms of violence and for whom violent acts are not a regular occurrence. However, most habitually violent teenagers do not learn from the natural consequences. They see their world as one continuous threat to their well-being that must be aggressively defended—with intimidation, a fist, a knife, or a submachine gun.

Some teenagers become engaged in violent activity by association with violent peers or gangs. Teenagers who would not otherwise engage in violent acts can find themselves caught up in constructing a groupthink psychology that permits and encourages violence. Sometimes, too, drugs and alcohol, ignorance, hate, or boredom fuel groupthink mentality.

Intercession

In today's world, it is easy to become desensitized to violence. Kids can be as jaded as adults. The best intercession is to teach your kids about violence. Teach them through the consequence rule that interpersonal violence is unacceptable and will not be tolerated. Teach them through your religious or moral values that violence solves nothing. Teach them that violence is wrong not just because it will lead to trouble, but because it is stupid. Any fool can pull a knife or a trigger. Any dolt can swear at people and threaten them. Any thug can beat up someone who is weaker. It takes someone with skill and courage and intelligence to settle differences with ideas, and to respect the ideas of others. Violence is the last refuge of the coward.

If your teenager needs further persuasion, spend a weekend night in the lobby of a big city hospital emergency room. Let him see what a knife or gunshot wound looks like in someone's chest, or someone who has been beaten senseless (some violence prevention programs for kids are providing videos of just such mayhem). Take him to the women's shelter and have him talk to battered women. Take him to the funeral of a teenager gunned down in a drive-by shooting. Finally, take him to the state prison system for juvenile offenders and have him talk to the kids who are incarcerated for violence. Suddenly, violence isn't as clean and simple and as exciting as it appears to be on TV.

Logical Consequences

The essence of the logical consequence is arranging for your teenager to attempt to put things back as they were before she committed the violent act. Confiscate and forfeit to responsible authorities any street weapons the teenager may have possession of. The teenager needs to pay the medical bills (or reimburse the insurance company) for victims of assault and injury. She needs to pay restitution to victims of property damage or make repairs. And she needs to make formal apologies to the court and to the victims.

If the juvenile law authorities are involved, these consequences should be in addition to the court-mandated sanctions. A number of juvenile courts have victim-offender reconciliation programs where the violent adolescent is required to meet with and pay restitution to the victim. This consequence is designed to help the teenager gain a personal perspective on violence, that it has a human face and causes suffering without reason.

Supervision

Pay close attention to the designated ratings on video games, CDs, and the movies that your teenager wants to rent or own. Are the language and the depiction of sexual activity and/or violence acceptable to you? If a video game is rated T (Teens) or M (Mature), what does that mean exactly? What is a "realistic" depiction of blood and gore? Ask to preview the material in the store. Set out written guidelines for your teenager to follow or block violent games on video consoles. Be especially mindful of the content in these forms of entertainment if your teenager is habitually aggressive. It only makes sense—the more aggressive the teenager, the less he should be exposed to violent content and images.

Using All Active Consequences

Intercede by arranging anger management, conflict resolution, drug treatment, and/or self-defense training (for kids who are afraid of being victims). Network with the adults in your teenager's life to get reports about violent behavior. Track for signs of violent activity; look for weapons, drugs, excess money, and signs of affiliations with gangs or cults. Inform the police or juvenile authorities as needed. That means you report every instance of a violent act or association. If that results in your child being arrested, incarcerated, and placed on probation, so much the better. Both he and you will then have access to help that can turn things around.

If your teenager has access to the Internet, track where he has been and what he has seen. There are sites that promote violent fantasy and behavior, sites ranging from hate propaganda to instructions for bomb making, to child pornography. Put blocks on these sites, install filtering software, and monitor your teenager's use of the Internet consistently. Monitor and supervise where your teenager is, what he is doing, and whom he is with as long as he demonstrates an interest in violence.

Dangerous Teenagers

Unfortunately, there are a very few teenagers who are seemingly "born that way"—that is, with an aggressive and violent nature. These teenagers have an underdeveloped moral conscience, crave weaponry, are spellbound by violent movies and games, hurt small animals and younger children, frequently threaten and assault others, and express no remorse. If you think these characteristics describe your teenager, have him tested by a psychologist and detained by the authorities if he commits acts of violence. Such teenagers need a high level of intercession to alter their behavior.

Protect Yourself

Finally, never let the violent adolescent get by with intimidating or using violence against you, the parent. If he or she pushes or shoves while swearing at you, report the adolescent to the police for harassment (offensive physical contact). If he or she hits you, it constitutes battery or assault. If he or she breaks things or punches holes in the walls, that is property damage or vandalism. Even if the police decline to detain your teenager, it is important to make the call so that there is a history of domestic disturbance calls involving your teenager. You want to be clear with your teenager that you will not tolerate such behavior.

Lock up or secure any weapons that you may have in the home, for your protection and others'. Learn self-defense skills (pins, holds, and blocks) that turn the violence back on the perpetrator. Take classes in martial arts such as Aikido that do not inflict pain and injury, but turn the aggression back on the aggressor. Usually one experience finding himself kissing the linoleum after taking a swing at Mom will be enough to dissuade even the biggest, meanest kid on the block from raising his fist again. Such self-defense skills can also be used with kids who have explosive tempers and may need to be temporarily and nonviolently restrained. Be aware that you *must* have formal training in these skills in order to prevent injury to yourself and/or your teenager. Contact law enforcement agencies for names and locations of approved training sites. The intent is not to cause harm but to prevent it.

Protect Your Teenager

Some teenagers turn violence upon themselves. Kids who talk about or attempt suicide or who carve or burn themselves are kids in deep emotional pain. Look for the warning signs (see "Early Warning Signs of Problematic Behavior"). You must always take any discussion or note writing about suicide or evidence of self-abusive behavior seriously and have your teenager assessed by a mental health professional. For actively suicidal kids, twenty-four-hour watches in a hospital or at home with follow-up therapy may be the best intervention. The same is true for mentally ill children who use violence to cope with their distress.

Finally, do not permit violence in your own life. If you or someone you love is violent, take immediate steps to correct it. All of the interventions discussed above can be used for yourself or your spouse or partner.

Peace is the natural order of things. Using these violence-prevention skills will promote the natural order of things. We can have peace in our families when there is peace in our homes.

CHAPTER TWENTY-SIX

WHEREABOUTS AND CURFEWS

Sample consequence rule:

- Observe all curfew laws.
- Be home for the night by specified times.
- Always ask permission before leaving one location and going to another.

Natural consequence: At risk for arrest, assault, or injury.

Logical consequence: Loss of out-of-the house freedom for a specified period of time.

Active consequences: Networking, monitoring, tracking.

A s children get older and feel a need for independence, they want to spend increasingly longer periods of time out of the house and away from their parents. This is as it should be. Most kids can handle the freedom and can make appropriate decisions for themselves. Such adolescents are rightly permitted to do what they choose and to come home when they like—within reason.

If you don't set a curfew for them, the city or county where you live has likely already done so. The reason is simply because it is not safe or desirable for kids to be out late without a legitimate reason, or unless they are under responsible adult supervision. In some communities, there are daytime curfew laws during the school day, as well as those at night. Like it or not, the government does regulate parenting to some extent. Since the government may step in, it is important that we know what the laws are in our community regarding curfew, and to make certain that our teenagers follow those laws.

Supervision and Networking

If kids are going to be out at night, possibly up to the time of the curfew, then they should be in "confined" areas: at a job site, in an approved home, at a movie theater or skating rink, at a Friday night football game, and so on, where there is at least some semblance of adult supervision. Kids are especially at risk while cruising on the streets or standing on street corners talking to their friends late at night. This is not to say that kids should never be allowed to congregate with their friends at night—it is to say that they are at greater risk for harm.

You may live in a community where drive-by shootings, drunken fights, robberies, rapes, and drug deals are nonexistent, or you may live in a community where they are common. These activities almost always happen under the cover of darkness and fear, and innocent teenagers can find themselves caught in the crossfire. It only has to happen once for your child to be maimed or killed.

Most juvenile crime (and sexual activity) takes place between the hours of three o'clock and six o'clock in the afternoon. Obviously, this is when most kids are out of school and away from adult supervision. If you have reason to believe that your teenager needs supervision to avoid trouble, consider enrolling him or her in after-school activities, or signing up for late-afternoon activities sponsored by programs such as the Boys and Girls Club or YMCA. Some churches and religious centers also offer supervised activities for your teenager.

If your teenager refuses to go, or you cannot find a suitable site, alert the network to keep an eye on things. Perhaps your neighbor will be willing to report comings and goings at your house. Or you can make arrangements with a trusted parent of one of your teenager's friends to help you. Some parents in networks agree to take turns in "patrolling" homes of kids in the network, driving by or ringing the doorbell to see what is going on. You can also hire a housesitter for the hours you are gone and can't supervise.

Should you ever compromise on curfew times? Compromise should be the exception, not the rule. Kids know, as in most things, that if you compromise once you can be persuaded to do so again. There is also nothing wrong with using common sense regarding curfew. Younger kids should have an earlier curfew than older ones, and irresponsible kids need a tighter curfew than responsible ones.

Preventative Supervision

What if your kid continually disregards curfew or sneaks out of the house at night? If you have an idea where your teenager might be, don't wait for him or her to come—go and get them. If you can, make phone contact and request that a trustworthy adult—such as the friend's parent—help ensure that they leave for home immediately, that is fine too.

If your teenager is in the habit of not telling others where he is going, require a name, address, and phone number that is *verified* before he can go out again. You might also consider putting your teenager on the level system (chapter 5) until he or she shows signs of improvement. If your teenager is one who habitually "forgets" what time it is, have her carry a pager or cell phone (at her expense for the devise or minutes purchased) so that you can electronically alert her when it is time to come home. Some parents have also used Global Positioning Systems (GPS) to track their teenager's whereabouts. These devices can locate a person's whereabouts within feet of where they are standing.

Should the teenager who habitually sneaks out of the bedroom window at night have a window that opens? You don't need iron bars and attack dogs, but you do need to secure the bedroom window from the inside. In certain cases, you can go so far as to have your teenager sleep in your bedroom at night in a sleeping bag, or you can install door knob alarms or home security systems to keep her in at night, but don't forget to have smoke alarms and exit plans for fire safety. Until when? Until the teenager's nighttime wanderlust ceases.

Monitoring

Finally, for the generally trustworthy teenager who needs to be home by a certain time, don't wait up late waiting for him. Make notifying you solely the teenager's responsibility. Here is how: tell them that you have an alarm clock set for his curfew time set just inside your bedroom door. It's his job to turn off the alarm before the curfew time arrives. If you are awakened, you will be grumpy when he gets home and may restrict him from going out again. Having to make a mad dash to turn off the alarm before it wakes you up may help the teenager learn to be punctual. If you think a sibling may be enlisted to turn off the alarm for the wayward teenager, a kiss on the cheek will do. If that would disturb your sleep, have your teenager leave his wallet and house keys by your bed.

For the generally untrustworthy teenager who needs to be home by a certain time, here is what you do: require him or her to take a photograph of him or herself using a digital or cell phone camera. The camera will record the date and time the picture was taken. Specify that the picture inside the house include some prominent feature in the background. If you think a wily kid will sneak back out of the house, leave the security system set to be activated a few minutes past the scheduled curfew time.

EPILOGUE
Every Good Thing

You now have two strong hands to work with to accomplish the behavior change you want to see in your teenager. On the right hand, you have discipline skills, contracting, and the point system. The discipline skills stop and prevent negative, unwanted behavior, and the reward systems encourage and strengthen positive, wanted behaviors. When used in tandem, the discipline skills and the reward system will quickly and effectively change behavior. However, the changes will not *last* without the skills of the left hand.

On the left hand, you have communication and problem-solving skills. When used in an atmosphere of love and praise, you will greatly strengthen the parent-child relationship.

Do not be tempted to put your emphasis on only one set of skills. Discipline without encouragement will not work; love without discipline will not work; and relationships without work will not work. To do that would be like trying to sit at a table where one of the four legs is too long or too short. The imbalance invites disaster. *When the skills of the right hand and the left hand are in balance, they work wonders.*

Parenting skills are like any other skill. You must practice them until they become a natural part of your being. If you do not see the behavior change you want, stay with it. Your teenager did not acquire negative behavior overnight and it will not change overnight. Change frequently arrives in small, incremental steps that can be celebrated and built upon.

Kids are as changeable as the wind direction. Change will come. The great thing about the strategies presented in this book is that you will see change before your eyes.

Let's say you have started a discipline plan to stop your teenager's drug use. You have established the consequence rule and provided intercession. You have begun tracking, monitoring, and networking with the adults in his life. You have communicated with him about your concerns and problem-solved strategies for him to say *no* to his friends and others. You have set a point system with rewards and praise for evidence of no drug use. You have shown him how much he is loved. The result is a decrease in drug use and abandonment of it in a short time.

Kids respond to their parents' demands when they see that their parents are serious about behavior change and will follow through consistently to make it happen. They respond to their parents' demands because they have a loving relationship that they value and do not wish to see disrupted.

I have a daughter whom I love with all my might. I know that you feel the same way about your child or children. Loving them with all our might means doing everything in our power to teach, guide, protect, nurture, direct, correct, and empower them to be and to have every good thing. Do practice the strategies and skills in this book. Your teenager will have every good thing come to them.

—*Michael Hammond*

SUGGESTED READING

Bodenhamer, Gregory. *Back In Control: How to Get Your Children to Behave*. New York: Fireside, 1983. (This older book details a number of useful ideas about parenting children with difficult behavior.)

Chamberlain, Patricia. *Family Connections*. Eugene, Ore.: Northwest Media, 1998. (This book contains several excellent examples of point system economies and level systems.)

Driekers, Rudolph, and Victor Soltz. *Children, the Challenge*. New York: Duell, Sloane, and Pearce, 1963. (This classic book in the parenting literature explains the origin of the concepts of natural and logical consequences.)

Focus Adolescent Services. (This online service is an Internet clearinghouse of articles and resources for parents of troubled and at-risk teenagers. See www .focusas.com/index.html.)

Kazdin, Alan. *Parent Management Training*. New York: Oxford University Press, 2005. (Dr. Kazdin explains common behavioral parenting techniques, some of which are presented for practical use in *Decisive Parenting: Strategies That Work with Teenagers*.)

Ketcham, Katherine, and Nicholas A. Pace, M.D. *Teens under the Influence: The Truth about Kids, Alcohol, and Other Drugs—How To Recognize the Problem and What to Do about It*. New York: Ballantine Books, 2003. (This thorough book can help parents sort out alcohol and drug problems.)

McKay, Matthew, Martha Davis, and Patrick Fanning. *Messages: The Communications Skills Book*. Oakland, Calif.: New Harbinger, 1995. (A classic book on improving interpersonal communication techniques.)

Pruitt, David, ed. (American Academy of Teenager and Adolescent Psychiatry). *Your Adolescent: Emotional, Behavioral, and Cognitive Development from Early*

Adolescence Through the Teen Years. New York: HarperCollins, 1999. (This book contains a number of articles about teenager development.)

Sells, Scott. *Treating the Tough Adolescent: A Family-Based, Step-by-Step Guide.* New York: Guilford Press, 1998. (Dr. Sells describes a strong behavior modification approach with oppositional adolescents.)

Walsh, David. *Why Do They Act That Way? A Survival Guide to the Adolescent Brain for You and Your Teen.* New York: Free Press, 2004. (This book explains what happens in adolescents' brains and how development changes affect their behavior.)

INDEX

acknowledgment, 102
active consequences, 28–49; needed, 44–47; at work, 47–49
affection, expression of, 102
arguing, solving the problem, 109–14
argument deflectors, 111–12
asking for what you want, 78–80

behavior, defiant. *See* teenagers, defiant-behaving
Bodenhamer, Gregory, 109, 111, 112, 152
broken record, 112

caring days/love days, 104
chore completion, solving the problem, 115–20
closed questions, 70–71
clouding, 113
coercion cycles, 82–86
communication, 66–86; blocks, 81–84; five "Bs" of, 66–69
community service, 23–24
confiscation and forfeiture, 22–23

consequences, escalating levels, 41
contingency contracts. *See* if/then contract
contracts, 59–65
conversation, social, 69–70
criticism, 97

Davis, Martha, 91
doing things together, 103, 124
driving, solving the problem, 121–25
drug and alcohol use, solving the problem, 126–33

early warning signs of problem behavior, 32–33
earning freedom, 42–44
echo technique, 76–77

family circle, 103–4
Fanning, Patrick, 91
feedback, 71–73
friends, solving the problem, 134–39

good faith contract, 61–62

Howard, George, 51

"I" statement, 77–78
if/then contract, 60–61
incentives: and contracts, 65; and the defiant teenager, 104–5
in-exchange-for contract, 61
information technology, solving the problem, 140–43
intercession, 31–33

Kazdin, Alan, 95
kids, gangs, cults, and negative peers, 37

laughter, 104
level systems, 50–55; permanent, 53–55; shorthand version, 55
listening: cues, 71; intentional, 89–90; with empathy, 103
logical consequences, 22–27
love and affection, twelve ways to show, 102–4
love-gram, 104
lying, solving the problem, 144–47

Masters, John, 79
McKay, Matthew, 91
Messages: The Communications Skills Book, 91
Meyer, J. Douglas, 51
minimal effective response, 79–80
misbehavior, occasional, 24
monitoring, 39

natural consequences, 21
natural and logical consequences at work, 24–27
networking, 33–36; chain, 36; sample script, 35

open questions, 70–71
overcorrection, 23

paraphrasing, 75–76
parent deafness, 81–82
partnership, between parents, 15–18
Patterson, Gerald, 82
point chart, examples of, 57, 59
point economies, 55–59
points, extra, 58
positive behavior, recognizing, 94–95
positive opposite, 95
praise, 96, 119; mixing with criticism, 97; mixing with feedback, 97–98; mixing with formal rewards, 98–99; mixing with physical affection, 98
problem behavior checklist, 16–17
psychological presence, 162

quid pro quo contract. *See* in-exchange-for contract

reasonable guidelines, 18–20
reinforcers, 93–105
response cost, 176–77
rewards: activity, 100; material, 100–101; social, 100; unconditional, 101–2
Rimm, David, 79
rules: clear, 10–11; definition of, 3–4; developing, 4–7; enforceable, 11; establishing a firm foundation for, 3–8; fair, 9–10; how many, 7; language when writing, 11–13; necessary, 9; representative, 13–14; sunset, 7–8; writing, 13–15; writing for teenager, 9

running away, solving the problem, 148–54

school assignments and homework, solving the problem, 155–60
script technique, 80
sexually active, solving the problem, 161–65
shadowing, 189–90
sibling fighting, solving the problem, 166–70
solutions, workable, 91
specific problem-solving, 87–89
spending time together, 103
sponge, 112
stealing, solving the problem, 171–74
straight talk, 73–74
supervision, 39–41; preventative, 40–41
swearing, solving the problem, 175–79

taking notice, 74–75
teaching, 103
teenagers, defiant-behaving, 28–30
television, solving the problem, 180–83
thank-you-gram, 183
tobacco use, solving the problem, 184–87
touch, 102
tracking, 38
truancy, solving the problem, 188–91

violence, solving the problem, 192–96

the wall, 112–13
whereabouts and curfew, solving the problem, 197–200

yes and no, balancing, 91–92

ABOUT THE AUTHOR

Michael Hammond, PhD, is a clinical psychologist and a licensed marriage and family therapist. He lives in Salem, Oregon, where he maintains a private practice and works as a therapist, consultant, and speaker. Visit his website at decisiveparenting.com.